THE STRANGE

JOURNEY OF

AMERICA'S

BILL GOLDBERG

with STEVE GOLDBERG

I'M NEXT

MOST UNLIKELY

SUPERHERO

CROWN PUBLISHERS   NEW YORK

Published by Crown Publishers, New York, New York. Member of the Crown Publishing Group.

Random House, Inc. New York, Toronto, London, Sydney, Auckland
www.randomhouse.com

CROWN is a trademark and the Crown colophon is a registered trademark of Random House, Inc.

Printed in the United States of America

Design by Lynne Amft and Robert Bull Design

Library of Congress Cataloging-in-Publication Data
Goldberg, Bill
    I'm next : the strange journey of America's most unlikely superhero / Bill Goldberg, Steve Goldberg.—1st ed.
        p. cm.
    1. Goldberg, Bill. 2. Wrestlers—United States—Biography. 3. World Championship Wrestling, Inc.—Biography. I.Title: The strange journey of America's most unlikely superhero. II. Goldberg, Steve. III. Title.

GV1196.G65 A3 2000
796.812'092—dc21
    [B]   00-055459

ISBN: 0-609-60780-4

10 9 8 7 6 5 4 3 2 1

First Edition

I'd like to dedicate this book to someone who has always been by my side and through years of dedication has asked only for simple love and companionship in return. I dedicate this book to my best buddy in the world . . . Barron.

Contents

chapter one

FLASHBACK

The world was a blur. All I could make out was the glare of the lights above the ring. As my senses were returning, Kevin Nash's leathery crotch came into focus. Using a real cattle prod was my idea. If I was going to lose, it was going to look as realistic as possible, but when I ate the voltage I knew why those big beasts were so cooperative. As the crowd started to chant "Goldberg . . . Goldberg . . . Goldberg," I lay there wondering what the hell I was doing flopping around the ring like a fish in a Speedo. I wasn't even really hearing the crowd—for the first time in my professional wrestling career, their rallying chant was wasted breath. The mighty Goldberg's 175-match streak was about to end. Something else was filtering into my brain, and I distinctly remember the words. "Whatever you do, do *not* become a professional wrestler."

Taking a shot from Kevin Nash.

You're Going to Be a What?

"Don't worry," I said to my girlfriend, Lisa, "becoming a wrestler is the last thing I'd ever do." As one of the original Diamond Dolls (the precursors to the Nitro Girls) of World Championship Wrestling, Lisa had escorted such luminaries as Ric Flair, Diamond Dallas Page, and Arn Anderson into the ring. She knew the ropes of professional wrestling, and she wanted to keep me out of the ring and away from the soap-opera-like atmosphere.

Two years later, I was recovering from surgery and trying to figure out my life when I figured a trip back to my college town of Athens, Georgia, would do me good. I hooked up with the boys, my former Bulldog teammates Scott Adams, Mack Burroughs, and Larry Brown, and resident redneck-turned-yuppie Blake Mitchel. We were sitting around Scott's house drinking beer and shooting the shit. Scott was flipping the channels, and somehow the TV wound up on professional wrestling. I said to them, "Wouldn't it be a trip if that was me up there in the ring?" "Yeah, right," said Scott, "I can see it now: G.I. Jew to the rescue. You could tie up your opponent in the figure four–skin!"

The longer I was away from football, the less confidence I had in myself. And without one vote of approval from someone I trusted, I wasn't going to become a professional wrestler. I picked up the phone and called my mom.

"You're going to be a WHAAAAT?" She sounded like Jerry Lewis in *The Nutty Professor*. "I'm going to be a wrestler, Mom, you know, like the guys on TV." She thought I was kidding, and I didn't really blame her. When I explained that I was serious, she asked me if I really thought that being a wrestler was an honest living. I couldn't give her a straight answer then, and I don't know if I could now.

I was really reluctant to call my dad to tell him that I was seriously considering becoming a professional wrestler. Not because I was nervous . . . I was embarrassed. Nervous is when you're sixteen and you ask to borrow your dad's Jaguar. Embarrassed is having him see you driving down Main Street in a clownmobile. As you can imagine, his mood was less than enthusiastic. "Does someone have a gun to your head? Why can't you go back and finish college?" was about all I remember from that conversation.

The next call was to my oldest brother, Mike, "the Machine." Mike and I have different agendas in life, to put it mildly. We want to end up in the same place but we've taken very different routes to get there. He's made a lot of money in the aircraft business, and throughout my life I've turned to him whenever I needed help. I was always trying to prove myself to Mike, but I seemed to come up a little short. Like the time I borrowed his four-door Jaguar and brought back a three-door.

He was not at all amused with my new career choice; in fact, he was speechless. Mike used to pay me a hundred bucks every time I sacked the quarterback in college, which wasn't much of a bonus, given my limited pass-rushing ability. I figured that maybe his silence meant that he was calculating what it would cost him to pay me *not* to become a professional wrestler. Trying to convince Mike that professional wrestling was a worthwhile endeavor was like convincing him that I could pilot one of his DC-8s on an intergalactic voyage.

I think they all thought that I was on drugs . . . and, in fact, I was. I was still taking methadone to ease the pain from the injury that ended my NFL career. I was down but not out.

I didn't call my sister, Barbara, because I knew that she would support me no matter what. After me, she was the next youngest in the family. I owe a lot to Barb—she deserves credit for helping me keep sane while I was growing up. She was the one who actually raised me when my parents were busy body-slamming their marriage into submission.

I saved the call to my brother Steve for last. He was my hole card and it was time to play out my hand. When I called him and told him that I had decided to become a professional wrestler, he responded by laughing hysterically. He wasn't laughing just because he thought it was funny (which it was). He was laughing because he was happy for me. In his own warped mind, he saw right away what a great opportunity it was, and I knew there was hope. "You'll be on national TV, and you won't be wearing a helmet, so millions of people will see your face every week. And what's really cool is that you won't have to deal with football coaches anymore . . . go for it!" Steve and I were on the same wavelength and his approval gave credibility to my decision. I also knew that if I screwed up, I could blame him.

I'm *Groin* to Have to Find a New Career

I was having a pretty good preseason with the Falcons in 1994, which for me meant playing more than four or five plays a game. I was the third-team swingman on defense, which meant that I was the last man to go in, after a lot of people went down. I wasn't first, second, or third string, I was the last available defensive lineman . . . period. I make a point to laugh about my pro-football career because it was less than stellar. Despite being six foot three and 275 pounds, I was undersized and slow, which is a bad combination in the NFL. Not to mention I was always hurt. Basically, I sucked . . . no, I didn't . . . yes, I did. What you should know is that I'm my own worst critic—football, wrestling, whatever. I have a very pessimistic attitude. Some may say this isn't healthy, and almost being a psych major, I know that. But still, this philosophy seems to keep me on top of my game. And as for my football career, at least I was there, which is more than most people who have ever picked up a football can say. And you know what? The happiness that I have right now is 90 percent due to the fact that I can reflect upon my experiences and laugh at them.

It was the last preseason game, and we were playing the Philadelphia Eagles. I was lined up at noseguard when the quarterback faded back to pass and I somehow got around one of the offensive linemen. I chased the quarterback, I dove for him . . . and I missed him completely. Just making it to the quarterback was a huge feat for me, considering that I only had one sack in the NFL and that one was taken away from me. I got up to continue my pursuit, and the offensive lineman I had outmaneuvered chased me down and ear-holed me.

Ear-holing: to score a direct hit on the side of an opponent's head, using the ear hole of his helmet as the bull's-eye.

WARNING: THE FOLLOWING CONTAINS GRAPHIC VIOLENCE!

The next thing I knew, I was at ground zero of a nuclear nut-sac explosion, and like my character Romeo in the *hugely* successful movie *Universal Soldier: The Return,* I sustained heavy damage. This may sound strange, but right after I got hit, the first sensation I had was that my testicles had been ripped off my body and flames were shooting out of the sac. I somehow played the rest of the game, but I knew that something was terribly wrong.

I told the trainer what had happened, and the following week I went to see the team doctor. The original diagnosis was epididymitis, which is an inflammation of the cord around the somewhere I'd rather not say. I eventually went to see two other team doctors and none of them could figure out what was wrong. And since the common treatment for unknown injuries in the NFL seems to be prescription drugs, I was prescribed various ones to deal with the injury. I played the entire season being masked by Toradol (a nonsteroidal, anti-inflammatory, postoperative painkiller) and Vicodin (hydrocodone, similar to codeine). Week after week I would practice, but I couldn't do pass-rush drills or run sprints. Oh, what a shame. As I mentioned, I wasn't the greatest pass rusher to begin with, so without practice I was even worse. I felt like a charity case, and on game day I was lucky if I was on the sidelines in uniform instead of street clothes. I just wanted to get through the season and roll the dice to see if I had a job the next year. Like anyone else, I did what I had to do to continue pursuing my dream.

With the Toradol shots I could run on Sundays, but when the medication wore off I was miserable. I couldn't do a simple sit-up, so I literally had to roll out of bed for about six months. Although I lived on pain medication and my injury was showing no sign of healing, I wasn't about to give up on the dream.

After the season, I did what any overachiever would do: I bull-shitted my way through the final physical. This, I thought, would give me a slight chance to come back the next year. The team doctor asked me if I was all right, and I told him yes, but unfortunately my groin still hurt. All of the doctors whom I had seen said that there was nothing wrong with me, and that was the basis for my eventually suing the team for workers'-comp benefits.

Shortly after my final physical, I received a phone call from my agent to inform me that I was on the supplemental draft list for the new expansion teams—the Carolina Panthers and the Jacksonville Jaguars. The next day I received a call from the Falcons and was told not to worry because I'd been taken off of the draft list. Of course I was greatly relieved . . . that is, until I picked up the paper the next day and read that I had been drafted by Carolina in the thirty-third round. That's professional football for you.

I still wanted to play football, so I had to find a cure for my injury. Fortunately, my father is an M.D., and through his research he found a specialist to check me out. I was referred to Dr. William Meyers, who was the Chief of General Surgery at Duke University Medical Centers. He listened to my symptoms and came to the conclusion that I had torn part of my lower abdomen away from my pelvis. This injury is mostly seen in soccer players, but Dr. Meyers had performed corrective surgery on a number of hockey players as well, including Claude Lemieux and Mikael Renberg. Dr. Meyers had perfected a method of reattaching the muscle to the pelvis. Without the surgery, I had no hope of returning to football, and even with the surgery, the odds weren't much better for a guy like me. Regardless, I felt like this was my only choice, so I went under the knife.

The surgery entailed attaching the frayed abdominal muscles to a mesh that was then reattached to the pubis, whatever the hell that is. On February 23, 1995, they put me back together.

After the surgery, I went home to Atlanta to recover and prepare myself as best I could for Carolina's upcoming minicamp in March. I was bummed to be leaving the Falcons, where I'd spent the last three years and just qualified for my NFL pension. I made some great friends on the team, including: Mike Gann, Scott Case, Tim Green, Pierce Holt, Jumpy Gathers, Moe Gardner, Rick Bryan, Jessie Tuggle, Chuck Smith, Jamal Anderson, and Terance Mathis. The list goes on and on, and because of them, my time with the team was not only bearable, sometimes I actually had fun.

I was scratching for everything I could get with the Falcons, and I knew that all things considered, the odds of my making a new team weren't very good at all. Realistically, the odds sucked. I would be competing with big-name free agents from around the league, along with top draft picks. At least it was an opportunity. When I reported to camp and found that my former L.A. Rams teammates Frank Stamms and Paul Butcher had signed as free agents, my fatalistic attitude changed. These two guys were good to me when I was a rookie with the Rams, and through the years Butcher and I had become good friends. Even though I was gimped and unable to do anything but rehab my lower body, seeing my old buddies rekindled the fire in me and made football somewhat fun again. The fire quickly fizzled, though, because during practice I was no more than a spectator. Day after day, I did nothing more than follow my tedious rehab schedule. Fact was, the team was hauling ass and I was going nowhere, since I couldn't even run in place. On April 20, I became a footnote in NFL history. Coach Dom Capers called me into his office, and we mutually concluded that my services were no longer needed by the team. I became the first player in Carolina Panther history to be released, so I packed my bags and hit the bricks.

I went back to Atlanta and crawled into a hole. My life as a human being was over for all practical purposes, and I might as well have spontaneously combusted. I was beaten. Like a University of Georgia defensive back in the mid-eighties, I was burnt toast.

As bad as I felt emotionally, my balls still felt worse. Every day it seemed as though someone was kicking me in the nuts, and some-how, dammit, I was going to make them stop.

Again thanks to my dad, I found Ursula Wessleman, M.D., at the Johns Hopkins Pain Clinic in Baltimore. I was a patient there on and off from August 1995 until December 1996, which was beyond a doubt the worst time in my life, but at least, according to one of the clinic's reports, "my penis was normal." I was given vari-ous combinations of painkillers and nerve blocks, and for a while I was taking methadone, which is used to get addicts off heroin. In addition, I was prescribed a combination of time-release

GENITAL EXAMINATION

The penis is normal. The testes are bilaterally descended. There is a left testicular mass which according to the patient is varicocele which he has had as long as he can think back. In the right scrotal content there is a small soft mass at the posterior aspect of the testicle which is painful on palpation. Also the patient reports pain on palpation of the posterior aspect of the right testicle near the base of the penis.

Oxycodone, which is the equivalent of morphine. I could seriously relate to Jerry Garcia and his "long strange trip" before he checked out for good.

The medication was making me crazy. I was walking around with fire in my eyes, and I felt like I was going insane. What lengths a man will go to to play a game. The only way I kept my sanity was throwing around as much weight as possible in the gym. I spent a lot of time at Main Event Fitness on Buford Highway in Atlanta, which is owned by professional wrestlers Sting and Lex Luger. (You're welcome, Lex!) I would come in, crank up the music on my headphones, ride the methadone, and train like a monster.

PLAN:

1. The patient will start methadone for pain control. He will start methadone at 5 mg q.h.s. for one day, then 5 mg p.o.q. for 12 hours for a second day and then increase the dose to 5 mg p.o.q. for 8 hours. The patient received a prescription today for a total of 100 tablets. The patient signed the opiate consent form today. He will call me on August 16, 1995, to discuss the effect of methadone on his chronic pain syndrome and possibly further titration of methadone.

2. The patient was instructed to call my office if he experiences side effects from the medication.

3. The patient will establish a primary physician in Atlanta with whom I can communicate in case the patient experiences side effects from the medication.

4. The patient will follow up in the Blaustein Pain Treatment Center in four weeks.

One day I was training at Main Event, and Lex, Sting, and Marcus Bagwell were there, working out together. While they were training, someone was making these annoying grunting sounds. Like the famous gorilla Willy B. getting it on with one of his new roommates at the Atlanta zoo. I thought it was Bagwell. In reality, it turned out that they were mimicking a little guy who was acting like a 135-pound bar weighed a thousand pounds. But because of the methadone, I thought they were making fun of me. In my infinite wisdom, I turned around and barked, "Blow it out your ass!" to the three of them. They stood there dumbfounded.

I can't say that this was the first time that the Goldberg look came out, because it had reared its ugly head on the football field, but this may have been the first time that Goldberg the wrestler emerged. I looked at them like they were my prey and I was within seconds of taking them all on. I was going crazy inside and I was looking to take it out on someone. I was like a rottweiler chewing gunpowder . . . like Dick Butkus hitting the quarterback as he envisioned the severed head bouncing down the set of stairs in *Hush . . . Hush, Sweet Charlotte.*

I assure you that the incident will never be forgotten by anyone involved. To this day, Sting still comes up to me occasionally and tells me to blow it out *my* ass, and walks away laughing.

Sting:

Lex used to do this funny thing while we were lifting. He'd pick up a really light weight—maybe a five-pound dumbbell or something. And when he'd pick it up he'd pretend he was a powerlifter, sound effects and all. He'd give the old *bip. Bip–bip-bip-bip–bip.*

Biiiiiiiip.

This one particular day, we were in the gym, and Bill was working out in there, too. We weren't paying any attention to him, and he wasn't paying any attention to us. I didn't even know him.

We were all in the dumbbell section, and Lex started to do the whole powerlifter routine. And then I heard what I thought was somebody saying "Blow it out your aaaaass!" and I looked up and I thought, *Did I hear that right? Who said that?* There was nobody else around but Bill. I asked Marcus, "Did you hear that? Did Lex hear that?" So I called over and said, "Lex, um, I think that guy's trying to say something to you."

Lex asked, "What, what, what?"

"I think he's telling you to blow it out your ass!"

I don't remember if we said anything. I think it was one of those situations where we decided to just leave him alone.

Apparently, Bill thought the *bip* stuff was directed toward him. He was just sure it was! Still, he stood right up to both the owners of this gym and another wrestler besides and told us "blow it out your ass!"

I thought to myself, *Wow, this guy's got some* cojones, *man!* He didn't tactfully say, "Excuse me, you guys got some kind of problem?" He cut right to the chase: "BLOW IT OUT YOUR AAAAAAAAASS!"

I needed time to recover, but I still thought that I could play in the NFL. Unfortunately, none of the teams felt the same way. Not a single team would return my phone call. I was faced with the reality that football was no longer a part of my life, and I had to figure out . . . WHAT'S NEXT?

I had no idea what to do because never in a million years did I imagine that I'd still need to make a living after playing pro football. I thought I'd play a few more years, retire from football, and be set for life. But the fact is, I retired a bit prematurely and I couldn't afford to wait twenty-three years to start collecting my pension. I never got the big paycheck, but I foolishly assumed that with one good season, I could get a contract that would set me up for life. I was set all right . . . for a couple of months. Soon I was living off of my credit cards, and when they maxed out I was down to using my dad's Phillips 66 card, which I put a lot of miles on in college. Thanks to Dad and the full-service Phillips 66 station, I always had Red Man, sardines, baloney, bread, eggs, crackers, and a lot of gas. Eventually, I was back on the phone to Mike looking for a handout. But this time was different. This time I was in a position that I was not accustomed to.

I always felt that I could do just about anything that I wanted to do as long as it had to do with football. That was my motto, and it was easy to live by because all I ever wanted to do was play football. I went to grade school, junior high, high school, and eventually college to do one thing: play football. And after college, it was the same thing. Since I never wanted to do anything else, failure was not an option. I didn't prepare myself in case something happened. I limited my choices because I limited myself. I had been drafted by the Rams and played with the Falcons in the NFL. I played a season with the Sacramento Surge in the World League and I even considered Canadian football. All that was left was the Arena League—playing for a cup of soup, a piece of bread, and twenty-five bucks a week was not my idea of a good time. To me, Arena football was the equivalent of jail time; playing football was over for Bill Goldberg.

I assessed my career options. My brother Mike offered to take me into his business, but I didn't know shit about airplanes except that I liked flying in them upside down. I had worked for him in the past, when I was rehabbing between stints with the Rams. Mike was doing me a favor by basically paying me to train. My job consisted of looking up jet-engine disk records and it was the most boring, monotonous, tedious, never-ending work I had ever done. He would let me come in late so that I could work out, and though I was never expected to wear normal business attire, it still sucked. Mike was very generous, but I was very independent, and I didn't want to have to work for him again.

Brother Mike and me in Miami, 1989.

I could learn to be a restaurant manager and work for my brother Steve, but he vowed to kill me if I ever got into the restaurant business. Although eating and drinking are two of my favorite pastimes, I heeded Steve's advice and never seriously considered this option.

I could have gone back to the University of Georgia and finished school, but I couldn't face the fact that I had gotten cut from pro football, and, in my mind, I was a failure. I thought that I'd be ridiculed because I was a loser at thirty, who wasn't good enough to keep playing football. So because of this foolish train of thought, school was definitely out.

I was getting back into shape, and I thought about becoming a personal trainer or a bouncer. As an ex–pro football player, I figured that I could command top dollar as a trainer, so I decided to give it a try. I coughed up 250 bucks to take the four-hour course and receive my personal-trainer certificate—which would be my first diploma since high school. There was only one problem: When I

got to the gym, reality hit me in the face and didn't pull the punch. The class was held at Main Event Fitness, and I was embarrassed to be back there. I didn't want all the people who knew me as a football player to see me taking a course to be a trainer. Nothing against trainers, but the final realization that my football career was over brought me down so low that my ass was scraping the pavement. But I had to do something. I had business cards printed up—*Body Mechanics, Bill Goldberg, President.* But I just couldn't bring myself to use them, and in the end, I only had one client: me.

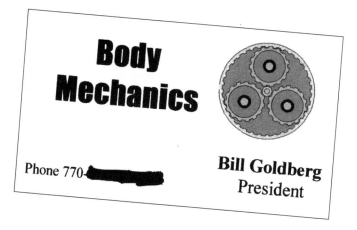

Looking at my career choices, you can see how far down professional wrestling was on my list. For a while, I wasn't very ambitious, and I didn't really aspire to do anything except to get off the couch. At the time, getting up to cook myself some eggs was a nine-to-five job. It wasn't like, "Hey, I'm going to get up today and go to school to get my MBA or become a lawyer." It was more like, "Hey, I'm going to get up and go work out and get a tan and maybe go be a trainer."

During my party years in Atlanta, I crossed paths with a lot of professional wrestlers, including Diamond Dallas Page, Scott Steiner, and Buff Bagwell. I had become friends with Sting and Lex through working out at their gym, and I knew Glen Gilbertti from the University of Georgia. I remember how excited he was when the

WCW dubbed him Disco Inferno, which to me sounded pretty goofy. One night in Atlanta, in a bar that is best left anonymous, my girlfriend introduced me to Eric Bischoff, then the head of World Championship Wrestling. Sometime later, I heard through the wrestling grapevine that Mr. Bischoff wasn't very impressed with Bill Goldberg the first time they met, and come to think of it, Eric Bischoff didn't do that much for me, either.

More and more, the wrestlers I knew tried recruiting me into wrestling, and looking back at it now, I understand why. We always try to improve our stable because you never know when the next big star will come along, and if one guy draws, we all draw. Diamond Dallas Page was the most persistent, but Sting and Lex were working me a bit, too (after we got past the "blow it out your ass" episode). Lex had played football for the University of Miami and also played in the NFL. In a way, I could relate to him. They seemed like good guys, and they were making good money, and my personal financial picture looked bleak, so maybe professional wrestling wasn't such a bad idea. But I still wasn't convinced.

Then one day I ran into Sting at his gym, and he invited me and my buddy Larry Brown to a NASCAR race in Bristol, Tennessee. Larry had gotten me into stock cars, so we took him up on his offer and went to the race. We noticed that Sting was as popular as the drivers, if not more so. I was impressed with what I had seen, but the thought of stepping into the ring was still embarrassing to me. I wasn't ready to put my future in the hands of some front-office wrestling guy who might dress me up as the mysterious missing seventh member of the Village People.

Sometime later Sting invited me to a match in Charlotte, North Carolina. He knew that I was potentially interested in wrestling, and he thought that it would be helpful for me to see what went on backstage. Possibly, I could hook up with Eric Bischoff again. I figured, what the hell, and agreed to go and check it out.

I drove to the match with Sting, his father, and Lex, and for three and a half hours they kept me entertained with stories from their bizarre world of professional wrestling.

We arrived at the arena the required six hours before show time and after checking in, Sting, Lex, Rick Steiner (Scott's brother), and Randy "Macho Man" Savage left to work out at a nearby gym, and I tagged along. This turned out to be my first road trip as a wrestler: I arrived at the arena with them; I left to work out with them; I came back to the building with them. I started to feel

Larry Brown and the crew in Bristol, Tennessee.

like one of them and it felt O.K. In the locker room they were playing cards and joking around, and it was the closest thing I'd seen to the camaraderie of playing football, which I sorely missed in my daily life. I was reintroduced to Eric Bischoff, and I expressed my interest in a wrestling career. Since his schedule was so hectic, he told me to call his office in about two or three weeks. Suddenly wrestling was becoming a serious possibility.

Diamond Dallas Page:

We met in Atlanta, and within twenty minutes we were doing shots. I'm saying, "You need to be in the business!" And he goes, "I'm really not into that business. I want to get that gold. I want to get that championship ring." He was all about football then! We became friends. We'd talk every once in a while. I'd see him in the gym, because you know the genetic freak he is, he was always working out. He had a tremendous work ethic when it came to trying to be in the best shape he could be. Anytime I'd see him I'd say, "So, you ready yet, bro?"

One day I saw him in Charlotte, and he walked in with Sting and Lex, and I pulled him aside, and I said, "So, what's the deal, bro? You thinkin' about it?" He said, "You know, things didn't work out with football, with my abdominal tear and all that stuff, so, yeah. I really want to talk to Bischoff."

Sting:

I wasn't really trying to recruit him, but I knew he was hell-bent on doing something. I think he was dissatisfied with football for a lot of different reasons. He was looking to do something else, and he had that look in his eyes that said he could do it.

Over the years, you talk to guys who want to get into wrestling, and you try to discourage them from it because you know, right off the bat, *This guy's never gonna make it.* Being a wrestler is more than just bleaching your hair and developing some kind of costume. It's way beyond that. I knew Bill could do it. He definitely had the look. Physically, he was absolutely perfect for it. He had the right voice. He was intelligent. He didn't have a shy bone in his body. He had all the tools that it would take.

The next day I was sitting around reflecting on my first voyage into the soap-opera world of professional wrestling. I thought about all of the time that I had spent with Sting. In his career, he'd been very successful and he'd done it the right way—he was a guy with integrity, and I thought, *If he can do it then why the hell can't I?* I really looked up to him. That's when I decided to use that number and give Eric Bischoff a call. And that's when I called my family to discuss my new career.

chapter two

It was early July of 1995, and I was passing time before calling WCW. When I spoke with Eric Bischoff in Charlotte, he said that he'd be on the road for three weeks and I should call him when he returned to Atlanta. I called when the time came, but the office said he wasn't around, so I left a message and my number.

He must have been gone a little longer than planned because after a week I still hadn't heard from him or anyone else from WCW. So I called him again and after another week without a response, I decided to give it one last try. When I didn't hear back, my next call was to the World Wrestling Federation.

Waiting every day for WCW to call was, in a way, reminiscent of my pro-football experience, except that it wasn't nearly as pressing. If you're an out-of-work football player, the closer you get to the season without a phone call, the less chance there is that you'll be playing. Fortunately, there isn't a professional-wrestling season . . . at least that's what I thought at the time. The fact that there is no season means that you can get a phone call 365 days a year. Conversely, looking back on it, that's the worst part of what we do because we don't get a break. Deep down, I still had hopes of playing football, and if some team had called me prior to my signing a wrestling contract, I would have jumped at the chance. At the time, I was hoping for a last-minute reprieve that would save me from a life of professional wrestling, but as luck would have it, the call never came. Even though I was more or less committed to becoming a wrestler, I knew

I could always do something else if wrestling didn't pan out. I could always wake up one day and decide to be ambitious.

Me with hair and my girlfriend, Lisa.

I was pissed off by the fact that I hadn't been contacted by Bischoff or WCW. I didn't think that it was good business to tell someone to call you and then never respond. But what do I know. I guess that's when I started figuring out about the so-called business side of wrestling. The World Wrestling Federation was my other option. I knew a guy in Atlanta named Jim Ross who used to work for WCW but jumped ship and went to work for the World Wrestling Federation. In addition to being in the wrestling business, he was a sports reporter in Atlanta, and like me, Jim was from Tulsa, Oklahoma. Jim had interviewed me when I was with the Falcons, but I hadn't talked to him since. I had nothing to lose, so I called him and inquired about possibly hooking up with the World Wrestling Federation. He arranged a meeting with them, and a week later I was on a plane headed to Stamford, Connecticut.

When I arrived at the World Wrestling Federation headquarters, I met with a number of people—from costume designers to members of the production staff. I remember thinking how surreal it was that I had come to the point where wrestling was actually becoming a reality for me. This was no joke. This was big business. After the lengthy tour, it was time to meet the man—Vince McMahon, the czar of professional wrestling himself. Vince was a smooth, authoritative, carnylike, car-salesman sort of guy. He was Vince McMahon, just like on TV.

We discussed a number of things, from the friends I had in wrestling to my commitment to my decision to wrestle. I told him that I was so committed that I was willing to start soon and get this thing going. I went on to tell him that I obviously had put a lot of thought into the decision, and I had a plan for my career. There I was, a pro athlete sitting with my arms crossed, pitching myself to the Don King of professional wrestling. Never in a million years would I have imagined this.

After making my pitch to Vince, I discussed my dealings with WCW and how pissed off I was that they weren't calling me back. I told him that I was losing respect for the company and Eric Bischoff. Vince must have been laughing inside, ready to pounce on a new prospect and reveling in the fact that he had a chance to keep a potential talent from WCW.

They offered me a contract on the spot, and Vince even inquired about my starting on the following Monday. This was only five days away! In the back of my mind, I still had hope that WCW would call, so I told them that I needed a little time to think it over. I thanked them for the offer and went back to Atlanta.

As you can tell, my first choice was to stay around Atlanta and work for WCW. If I chose the World Wrestling Federation, I'd have to move to Stamford, Connecticut, and find a new place to live. This was a very important factor for me because for the first time in my life, I wanted to buy a house, and that decision was huge. All along, I had assumed that WCW was going to get back to me, so thanks to a loan from my mom, I was already involved in buying a house in Atlanta. If I decided to go up north, I would have to postpone the purchase. I was sick and tired of renting, so I really wanted a place of my own. I also didn't feel comfortable venturing out into this profession without allies. After all, most of the guys I knew were with WCW.

I was going back and forth with the World Wrestling Federation for about a month, all along waiting for someone from WCW to call. But finally I decided that I had put the World Wrestling Federation off long enough, and I didn't want to lose the opportunity. I had been dealing with Vince's wife, Linda McMahon, and I called her to make the final arrangements. On Thursday, at high noon, I was going to commit to a contract with the World Wrestling Federation and do my damnedest to become their next superstar.

But I guess it wasn't meant to be. The night before I was going to commit, out of the blue I received a phone call from Howard Bush. Howard was my agent in the NFL. He asked me how things were going with WCW. I said, "WCW? Those bastards didn't call me back," and I proceeded to tell him the whole story. He asked for their number so that he could call them on my behalf. Howard is a great guy, plain and simple, and with my limited ability as a football player, it was hard to determine just how good of an agent he was. All I know is that we were never able to reach my unrealistic goals. I didn't need a wrestling agent at that time, but I had nothing to lose. And besides, I figured there was no way they were going to call *him* back.

I'll be damned if they didn't. The next morning at nine o'clock, I got a call from Eric Bischoff. Go figure. So I've got to give credit where credit is due. Was it sheer coincidence? I don't know, but however it happened, thanks, Howard. I don't know how instrumental you were in their finally calling but, hey, maybe it couldn't have happened without you.

Eric wanted to talk about the possibility of my involvement with WCW. But to me, time was of the essence. I had to get something over the phone from Bischoff that was strong enough of a commitment for me to cancel with Linda McMahon before noon. During our conversation, I told Eric that I had no desire to be some five-hundred-dollar-a-week, throw-your-ass-around-the-ring, dress-me-up-in-a-clown-suit dipshit. Looking at wrestling objectively, I felt as though I could come up with a character that I thought people would like—someone powerful, explosive, and exciting. And more than anything else, I wanted a character partially based on who I really was. I thought this could really sell. I went on to explain my feelings to Bischoff: "To be perfectly honest with you, I can survive without wrestling. Realistically, my brothers are very successful, and I could work for one of them at the drop of a hat, but that's just not what I want to do. I've chosen to do this because I think I can contribute to the profession, and somehow I think it can be a lot of fun." Even though I knew nothing about the business, I felt that with my drive and determination, I would succeed. And if not, at least I would have tried. He went over some very basic contractual elements, and it wasn't long before we came to an agreement that opened the door to WCW. Aside from the actual decision to become a wrestler, that was the biggest decision of my life. I don't know what would have happened to me if I had signed with the World Wrestling Federation, but I came within only three hours of finding out.

Goldberg's Wrestling Philosophy

Almost everyone knows that in professional wrestling, the outcome is predetermined. From the beginning I wanted to be the guy who was cheered. Like when I played football, I wanted to be the defensive lineman who broke through the line and made the tackle. If I was going to wrestle, then I wanted to be one of the good guys. I wanted to be that indestructible superhero who could fly through the air and knock five guys out with a single punch, a guy that everyone could look up to. It would be cool to be Superman. What kid didn't grow up wanting to be Superman?

Now that I'm evolving as a wrestler, I have learned that not only can you perform well enough for the fans to cheer for you, but you can also perform well enough for them to boo you. That is a statement that I never would have understood in the past.

As for winning or losing, my philosophy always was and always will be that I don't care about the outcome as long as my integrity doesn't suffer. I don't care if I get pinned by Tiny Tim or the Elephant Boy. It wouldn't bother me if I were asked to lose a match to *anybody*, if I thought it was in the best interests of the show and it was realistic.

I am very competitive, but the wrestling business isn't about winning or losing; it's about entertaining. This attitude is contrary to the philosophy that was force-fed to me in sports, but in wrestling, losing to someone doesn't compromise your integrity or your worth as a man. If the Elephant Boy was a good wrestler, then I'd be losing to a good wrestler, not to mention a human oddity.

Money for Nothing

WCW's contract called for me to train for a certain amount of time until I was ready for my first match. I would work out five days a week for what I thought was less than a decent paycheck but at the time, it put me back on the map. I had a job again. It was early September when I signed the contract, and Eric told me that they would let me know when to get started. Several weeks went by, and I didn't hear from them (see a pattern here?), but the blow was cushioned because I was receiving regular paychecks for just sitting on my ass waiting for their instructions. I called them week after week until December 15, when finally the phone rang, and it was Terry Taylor from WCW. "Is this Bill Goldberg?" he asked.

"Yes, it is," I said.

"Well I just got a call from Eric Bischoff, and he asked me how you were coming along, and I told him that I hadn't the faintest idea who you are because you're not here."

I said, "Terry, I've been calling WCW every week since I signed my contract in September, and you're the first person to call me back." In amazement, he told me that he would get back to me with a time to report to their training facility, the Power Plant.

I hadn't trained one day, and I got paid for three months. How crazy is that? You know what else is crazy? Eric Bischoff didn't have a clue about my early dealings with the World Wrestling Federation and how close I had come to signing with them.

Wrestling has provided opportunities that football never gave me. In that respect, I owe a hell of a lot to wrestling, but by no means do I think that it's a perfect business or that everything is always rosy. Don't get me wrong, I may make fun of wrestling, but it doesn't mean that I don't appreciate the fact that I made the decision to become a pro wrestler, and I've prospered greatly because of that decision. It's just that wrestling can be a very goofy business. I mean, look at its origins. It evolved from the carnivals. Even to this day it's a circuslike business where the rules and regulations are made up as you go along, and it's every man for himself. It just happens that I chose to work for the WCW's freak show and not the World Wrestling Federation's . . . and it was show time!

chapter three

THE POWER PLANT

The decision was made. I was going to WCW, and the final step had to be taken—the step into that ring for the first time. At last Terry Taylor called me with a time to begin my training and directions to the facility. I didn't know what to expect when I walked into that run-down building because gathered there were some of the strangest-looking guys I had ever seen. If these people were on a football field, it would have been like a scene from *The Longest Yard*. They looked like a bunch of misfits, and they just weren't my type of guys. It wasn't my kind of scene. All you had to do was look into their eyes, and you could tell who was going to make it and who wasn't. Fear has a funny way of distinguishing itself, and you can't hide it at the dreaded Power Plant.

It was located near downtown Atlanta, an hour's drive from my house, and I made that drive five days a week, for seemingly forever. I was miserable for months, and the one thing I could always count on was a painful ride home. The head trainer there was a guy by the name of Dewayne Bruce, A.K.A. Sarge, and he was a stern, authoritative, overbearing, short little son of a bitch who packed a lot of punch. He was reminiscent of an army drill sergeant, and he put guys through hell. I knew, walking into the Power Plant, that there were a lot of unknowns, but the one thing I expected to find was a guy like Sarge. As a football player, I'd been up against some of the toughest, meanest, and strongest guys in the world of sports, and I swore to myself that no wrestler or trainer—or any man, for that matter—was going to make me quit. No matter how tough it was, I went through everything with a smile on my face.

Me, Sarge, and Bam Bam Bigelow—what a crew.

Sarge

Sarge is the wrestler-walking-off-the-street's worst nightmare, because he takes his job very seriously. He was an amateur wrestler, and he is a very basic individual with simple philosophies that he thinks will always work. He takes a lot of pride in what he teaches, so when a guy comes in off the street and thinks he can jump in the ring and start wrestling right away, Sarge is going to bury his ass. I knew that it was going to be a challenge when I first met him, but once I saw what he was all about, I felt confident that we would become good friends. Sarge instantly earned my respect. I knew that he would push me, and I wanted to show him that I would always be there to push him back. And Sarge liked to be pushed. When he came up with a new move for me, he insisted on being the guy I practiced it on. He wasn't satisfied until he felt it. He even seemed like he enjoyed having me do it to him. It sounds like a sex thing, but we never got it on, although I did pin him once or twice.

Sarge probably would have been a famous wrestler himself, but unfortunately, he is too small. He's five-foot-not-very-much, and in wrestling, being short is your worst enemy, because it more than limits your opportunities. You can make a person wider, but you can't make them taller, and needless to say, Sarge had been on the short end of the stick when it came to his rise as a pro wrestler. He wrestled as the Leprechaun in the Dungeon of Doom, and he wore a green suit into the ring. He was also Sergeant Buddy Lee Parker of the Georgia State Patrol. It's unfortunate that his magical powers and his law-enforcement authority couldn't add a few more inches to his height, because with his attitude, work ethic, and heart, he would have made a lot of money. These days he still wrestles, but rarely on TV.

His job was to train people for the future. Jody Hamilton, A.K.A. the Assassin, was the head of the Power Plant, and Sarge was the head trainer. Dewayne takes a lot of pride in bringing people into the new generation of wrestling. He's the one that molds the pieces of clay and turns them into wrestlers like Diamond Dallas Page, Big Sexy Kevin Nash, and Paul Wight (the Giant/the Big Show).

Sarge doesn't get a lot of credit, but he deserves it. I wouldn't be where I am today without Dewayne Bruce, and I also wouldn't be where I am if it weren't for Sarge. He's the guy that has been there for me since day one, teaching me not only about the wrestling part of the business but about the backstage part as well.

Sarge:

In any business, any show-type business, any TV business like the NFL or major league baseball, there's a lot of political backstage stuff that goes on. I've been here a lot of years, so I was able to help Bill out as far as "smarting" him up on a lot of things. Some people play mind games, and some people don't. I respect Bill so much, and with his work ethic, I figure I owe it to him. I knew he could make it. I knew he had it, and I just wanted to see him get it!

One thing Sarge and my parents taught me was to be nice to everybody because you see the same people on your rise to the top as you do on your fall to the bottom. Sarge has been the guy who has always been there for me in the ring, to teach me and toughen me up. He's the one that rides my ass, and he's always there for me twenty-four hours a day if I need to ask something about wrestling or just want to talk. To this day he'll pick up the phone and call me about moves.

Sarge is a guy I'll go out of my way for at any time, because he's a great family man with a great work ethic, and he wants nothing more than to succeed in the business and contribute. I recall a number of times when Sarge was, in more ways than one, treated unfairly. Once, when he was setting up a ring for *Monday Nitro,* he was really sick, but he refused to go home until the job was done. He caught walking pneumonia, and he didn't have medical coverage. He has three kids, and he works his ass off, and he's done it for a number of years. He is a very important person to the company. But Sarge isn't the kind of guy to go asking for help. And his hospital bills would have been a real burden for him financially. I went to Eric Bischoff to tell him about the situation. Fortunately, he came through and WCW took care of him.

Not everyone who wrestles for WCW has to go through the Power Plant. There are other wrestling schools, and there are guys from other federations who usually get a tryout during "dark matches"—matches that are performed in front of a live audience at a TV taping but not televised. Obviously guys like Dennis Rodman and Karl Malone don't go through the Power Plant, and fortunately, as a professional athlete I was brought in under different circumstances, too. What I had to do wasn't nearly as tough as what the normal tryout victims off the street were put through, and for that I'll always be thankful. But I still had to do hundreds of free squats and diamond push-ups, and we did a lot of running from ring to ring.

Sarge:

I put 'em through hell! The road's not easy! The first thirty to forty-five minutes to an hour, we're doing nothing but squats: Hindu squats, up-and-downs, grass drills, push-ups and stuff. I've got a whole routine designed where it's nonstop. The only break they get is lunch. They get an hour and that's it. I've had lots of guys leave their stuff. They say, "I'm getting sick. I've got to get something out of my car." They never come back to get their stuff, and they just take off. I've been known many times to follow a guy into a bathroom and pull him out. He better be puking! I don't punish one guy; I punish the group. I try to motivate people! It's easy to say, "I quit."

You had to practice hitting the ropes repeatedly, and if your ribs weren't cracked, it sure felt as if they were. Running up against the ropes was brutal because they are made of steel cables. I do it all the time now, and I'm conditioned to it, but back then, it was foreign to me, and I fought through it every step of the way. Your back would hurt like hell from doing bumps on the mat and from guys dropping you the wrong way. You'd get dropped on your head and hit full on because after all, these guys didn't know the right way to do the moves yet. The guys that could do them and make them look graceful earned my respect because they were a lot harder to do than I thought they would be.

I remember a conversation that I had with Lex and Sting before starting my training. We were working out at their gym, and we were talking about the steps that I'd have to take to become a wrestler. Sting mentioned that I'd have to go to wrestling school. "What?" I said. "Are you kidding me?" I thought it was a joke. I said, "I'll go for maybe two or three weeks." And then Sting looked at me like, "Well, I don't think you know what you're getting into." Obviously, after all I had to go through at the Power Plant, I sure as hell didn't know. After two or three weeks at wrestling school, I was still learning how to bounce off the ropes and recovering from bruised ribs.

At the Power Plant, they knew that I came from the Atlanta Falcons, and they knew that I had an advantage over the other guys because I was a proven professional athlete. As far as my ability to be a wrestler was concerned, they didn't know anything about that, nor did they know about my ability to blend in with their fraternity. They'd see a football player and they'd be personable to him, but they also had a chip on their shoulder. They wanted to prove that wrestling is hard work, that an athlete from another sport can't just come in and do it. So physically they'd put you through a certain amount to see what you were made of, but at least they wouldn't try to kill you like they would a guy coming in off the street.

Sarge:

I've had plenty of football players. In fact, my truck has got a lot of damage done to it by ex-football players that said they were big and tough and then after the tryouts, they were begging to leave. They decided to take it out on my truck when they left.

We had a pro-football guy come in here—six-eight, 330–340. He shook my hand and said, "You look a lot taller on television." I said, "O.K. Get on your stuff and let's get going." Thirty minutes later, he puked and I made him wipe it up with his shirt. He lay on the floor for an hour and then made his way to the office. He said he had an all-new respect for wrestling and that he was leaving.

They destroyed a lot of people at the Power Plant. All sorts of people walked in the front door thinking that they could make it as a wrestler, but what they didn't realize was that minutes later, many of them would be exiting that same door with shattered dreams. The trainers would ride these guys mercilessly, and it appeared that their objective was to take the guy's three-thousand-dollar fee, or whatever they charged, and see how quickly they could get them to quit. If a guy left in five minutes, he'd lose his money, his pride, and generally his chow.

When a new group would try out, we would observe and try to guess who would quit first. It was quite sadistic, the way we watched those guys going through hell and cheered for the first guy to fail. You could tell by looking at them who would make it, and I knew that I had an advantage because in football I had been through years of people trying to tear me down. This was no new challenge for me, but it broke a lot of other people right before my eyes. Once a month, CNN or *Extra* or E! would film the carnage for all the world to see, and the camera caught a lot of guys running out the door screaming and crying.

Learning the Ropes

Looking back, the physical part amounted to only about 50 percent of the training, and the rest was character development and what to do in the ring. Once they weeded out the people that couldn't handle the workout, they started to actually teach us how to become professional wrestlers. There were a lot of guys in different stages of their training, and the ones who had been in the class for a while would help demonstrate the moves. Every time a guy made it past the tryout stage, they would add him to the class, and he went along at his own pace until he was plucked out and used in a dark match. And therein would lie the beginning of his career. Some of the guys were in the class for a year before they got the opportunity. In most cases, they were paid very little, but they stuck with it because they wanted to fulfill their dream of becoming a professional wrestler.

The first thing you were taught was the lockup, and from there you learned the basic holds. From the lockup you learned how to go to a headlock, and then you learned how to work a guy's arm. Then you learned the basic moves: the snap mayor or snapmare or something like that (I don't know how to spell it or use it), the body slam, the fireman's carry, and the arm drag. The first submission hold that Sarge taught me was the cobra clutch, and the only time I ever used it was on the finish with Sid Vicious in our match in Toronto. What's a cobra clutch? Well, it could be the way you grasp a deadly snake or that left pedal in one of Carroll Shelby's sports cars, but in wrestling it's a submission hold. I'm not exactly an expert as far as wrestling holds. I know the basics, no question, because you have to have a basic understanding of what you're doing in the ring. But as far as people's finishing moves and knowing them by name, well, I know how to get out of them, and that's enough for me.

After you learn the basic holds, you learn combinations of moves so that you have an understanding of how to create some kind of a flow in the ring. Slowly, they teach you how to do a match in segments and spots, which are a series of moves. Then, you put the series of moves together in a logical order. You have a "heel" (bad guy), a "baby face" (good guy), a time limit, and a story. When you determine how long you want to tell the story, you can figure out your spots. There is a certain strategy to the match, and you try to combine spots to keep the fans on the edge of their seats. The goal is to take them up and down like a roller coaster.

Different people have different ways to plan a match, and a lot of the experienced guys can go in the ring and not plan anything at all. They just talk to you during the match, and they tell you exactly what they're going to do in very short ways. Two guys that have wrestled each other a lot can get in the ring without saying a word in the back and maybe say six or seven words and have a great match. They'll just feed off of each other until they get lost or finish the match. I get lost a lot. People think that I'm having a great match, when in reality I'm being carried the whole time, and the other guy is actually making me look good.

Sting:

I remember working with Bill. He would be all ears, and he'd listen to how we'd want to lay out the match. He might offer some advice, and I might say, "No, Bill, that doesn't make sense" because of whatever. He was really good about listening and I remember a couple of times he'd say, "I'll do anything for you. Anything you want, I'll do it!"

No offense to Sarge or anyone else who taught me, but to this day, I don't think that I have the ability to put together a logical match. My knowledge of wrestling is quite limited, and my knowledge of setting up a match is even more limited. I do what I have to do in the ring, and I feel as though I've done a good enough job to provide some decent entertainment for the fans. My idea of an exciting match is to step between the ropes, endure a certain amount of punishment, shake it off, and run somebody over.

There are also nonverbal signs in the ring, and one well-known example is giving a guy "the iggy." "The iggy" is a common term in the wrestling world for reversing a move. Just squeeze your opponent's arm, and he takes over. But you have to be careful because if you squeeze his arm the wrong way, he may want to make you his tag team partner.

Of course, in the old days, if I was telling you all this, there would be guys out there trying to break my legs because I'd be divulging the secrets of the business—secrets that seem ridiculous today. Now it's a different story. It's common knowledge that professional wrestling is not a sport—it's sports entertainment. Vince McMahon said so on national TV. Judging by their behavior, many pro-wrestling fans missed Vince's proclamation.

I trained for three months before my first real match. I went down to Universal Studios in Orlando where they taped all the Saturday night shows. We would go down there for about ten days every three or four months, and we didn't know how good we had it until it was taken away from us.

For me, going to Orlando the first time was very nerve-racking because I was under a lot of pressure to do well and start out on the right foot. Already it was better than football. Hell, I was right next to Disney World. We would wrestle from nine in the morning until two or three in the afternoon, and we had the rest of the day and night off. When I was done for the day, I would take off in my car and drive to Daytona Beach and lie out on the sand. I was a fool because I thought that this was what a real road trip was going to be like, and it couldn't have been further from the truth. This was a vacation compared to what I was about to embark upon.

We'd go match after match after match, and I had the opportunity to learn from quite a few people. That's why Orlando was a good training ground for me. They had main-eventers and guys just coming from the school. They brought in most of the stable of wrestlers, and there must have been a hundred guys performing taped matches for the next month's Saturday night shows.

Finally, it was time for my first match in front of a live audience, and I remember wondering to myself, *Am I good enough? Am I ready?* And then I realized that it was too late to question myself, because I was looking at Sarge across the ring. The bell rang, and then Sarge rang my bell. After a series of forearm after forearm after forearm and kicks to my head . . . kicks to my ribs . . . and kicks to every part of my body, the rest of the match was a blur. The next thing I knew, I woke up to the sound of the bell as I was declared the winner of my first match.

chapter four

THE PRODUCTION
OF GOLDBERG

When you complete your training and you're ready to start your career as a professional wrestler, you need to establish your identity, or, as they say in the business, your "gimmick." You are either given the idea for a gimmick, or, as in my case, you can attempt to develop your own character. The idea is to come up with a persona and a finishing move that sets you apart from other guys. The gimmick incorporates your style and look and body type. When you start wrestling in front of the public, you *become* the character you are portraying. Some people come in with their character already established from another federation, although that federation may own the rights to the character. For instance, the Big Show of the World Wrestling Federation used to be the Giant when he was with the WCW.

Three or four months before I started my training, I studied wrestling tapes and ordered Shoot Fighting and martial-arts tapes to look for new moves.

Shoot Fighting n.: A hybrid sport combining Muay Thai kickboxing and submission wrestling or jujitsu.

I developed my character mostly from the Shoot Fighting tapes, but I also incorporated moves from the martial-arts classes that I took when I played football. I figured that I could come up with something that people wanted to see. By watching a lot of No Holds

Barred tapes, I saw different styles of fighting. I figured if I could duplicate the moves in the wrestling ring without killing other people or myself, that it would be entertaining, not to mention quite violent.

I learned ways to incorporate fighting styles of people like Oleg Taktarov, who was a master of Russian sambo, a submission-fighting technique taught in the Russian army. I watched guys lay holds on people from the strangest positions, and I thought if I could do that, being as big as I was, with the look that I had, I'd be doing things that no one had ever seen before. Hopefully, this would create a lethal and electrifying package. I also wanted to use my size, strength, and tenacity from football in my character. As far as wrestling is concerned, I'm very lucky to have been born me, which I could never say in regard to football. Some people, including Vince McMahon, have called me a Steve Austin clone. This is not true at all, and I didn't care what Steve Austin looked like because in no way, shape, or form did I try to emulate him or anyone else. This isn't taking anything away from Austin because he has created a terrific character, and I respect him as a wrestler and as a person. Other people have suggested that my character was an attempt by the WCW to create a character similar to Ken Shamrock. This isn't true. Shamrock is a real Shoot Fighter and he brings the reality of Shoot Fighting to the world of professional wrestling. I'm just assuming a Shoot Fighting character, and the idea to do that was just something I came up with. I definitely wasn't copying Shamrock. I didn't even know about his wrestling gimmick. Wrestling is such an individual endeavor that if you copy someone else's character, it's obvious, and it means that you have no imagination whatsoever.

In football it's an entirely different story, because you're not allowed to use your individuality, and there are only so many ways to succeed. That's why I respected Howie Long and wanted to be like him. To me, he was *the man!* I have since met him, and he has even impressed me more as a person than he did as a football player. That's really saying something.

In something as silly as professional wrestling, which isn't based on athletic performance alone, success comes down to your ingenuity, and I figured that I could be as ingenious as anyone when it came to developing my character. I could choose any character I wanted, and I thought that by accentuating my own personality and multiplying it maybe times ten, I could create a good persona. I always knew in my mind what I wanted to do. I just let it evolve and kind of played it by ear and molded it myself within the leeway I was given. I wanted to avoid all the usual wrestling self-promotional hype. I wanted to be silent and carry a big stick (so to speak). If the crowd liked it, I'd be in. With a little bit of luck and the right finishing move, I'd be on my way to success . . . and hopefully, a lot of money.

The Goldberg Look

My girlfriend, Lisa, always thought that the bald-headed biker look was sexy. Since I already had the high and tight cut from football, I was already close to fulfilling at least one of her fantasies. One day, when I was recovering from my surgery, I felt like doing something crazy, so I grabbed a razor and took out a row of my hair. I couldn't go back so I finished the job, and I've been bald ever since. It was well before my wrestling career, right after I got out of football. I was in the mood to do *something* then because there wasn't much else going on. It wasn't like I was going to work at a law office every day.

As far as the motorcycle was concerned, since I was a kid I always wanted to ride one, but because my dad was a doctor, it was out of the question. He used to tell me that if I wanted to get a bike, he would take me down to the emergency room to show me what happened when you crashed on a motorcycle. If I could walk out of there and accept the fact that it could be me all mangled up, then he would consider it. It wasn't until I wrestled for the *Road Wild* pay-per-view in Sturgis, South Dakota, that I got my first Harley—a Road King.

It seemed that there was one thing missing to complete the look, and that was a tattoo. Deep down, I had always wanted a tattoo, and it was just a matter of time before I gave in and inked the deal. Lisa had introduced me to a tattoo artist named Mike Parsons, just in case I ever decided to get one.

So one day I was just sitting in my house not planning to get a tattoo . . . just like I wasn't planning on shaving my head and wasn't planning on becoming a wrestler. I was thinking, *Hell, if I follow through with all of these changes, then maybe I can't back out of the decision to become a wrestler.* That's when I got the tattoo. I was so reluctant to become a wrestler that I tricked myself into doing it, honest to god. I shaved my head and wrestling was closer to reality.

I got the tattoo and wrestling was closer to reality. I kept doing these things until I couldn't turn back without looking stupid. Thank god, I didn't get a nose ring.

I had seen a guy in a No Holds Barred competition who had a tattoo that caught my eye. There was just something about it that was different—and I am a man who likes to be different. Something made it stand out; I don't know if it was the points or whatever, but it stuck in my mind. When I was working on the set of the movie *Ready to Rumble,* there were two fighters in the ring messing around, and I started talking to one of the guys. I'll be damned if it wasn't the same guy that I got the idea of the tattoo from. Sorry, dude, but yours looked like shit. I'm glad I never saw a close-up of it because I never would have gotten my tattoo.

I just happened to be in the neighborhood the week before, and I went to Psycho Tattoo and showed Mike Parsons my idea. He told me it would cost $375 for what I wanted, and a week later I just happened to have 375 bucks in my pocket. I figured, *Hell, I'm in the right state of mind; I might as well do it.*

So I drove the thirty minutes to Psycho Tattoo and picked out a design that was similar to the one I had seen. With a little coaching, Mike started drawing it freehand, and he molded it to the size of my shoulder. It was intricate—he measured everything and did it strategically.

I had some time to kill before he was ready to get started, so I went down the street to a restaurant. I ordered some chicken-fried steak, and I had two or three shots of tequila and some beers. I still had enough time to go down the street to where Lisa was working, and I went in and told her that I was about to get the tattoo. She was surprised and very happy with my decision.

It took three and a half hours, and it didn't hurt nearly as much as I thought it would, but all of the alcohol in my system thinned my blood and I bled like crazy. My shoulder sizzled like a porterhouse on the grill. I kind of enjoyed it.

I remember when I showed up at my cousin Jane's wedding in Omaha with a bald head and a tattoo. The reaction from the family was less than favorable, but I didn't care what people thought. I just went with it. I knew that I had an idea, and I knew that if that idea was brought out and thought out and followed through, I could succeed.

The Uniform

Before my first match I was standing outside of the trailer when one of the bookers, Paul Orndorff, came over to talk to me. Paul was one of the wrestlers I had watched as a kid, and I always liked him. He suggested that I shave my body hair to show off more muscle definition. I kind of went along with it with a quick "Yeah, O.K.," but I wasn't about to shave because I wanted to look like a football player looks, as opposed to a cut bodybuilder. The guys that I knew who shaved their bodies were all bodybuilders, and I thought it was kind of fruity. Of course, now I shave my back and everything (well

almost everything), and I'm not a fruit, so whatever. . . . I like fruit.

I did everything I could to get away from wearing briefs. I wanted to wear a wrestling singlet,
football pants, or something. I was digging for
anything to not have to wear my underwear out
there. Terry Taylor talked to me about wearing
shin pads in the beginning so that I'd look like
some of the Shoot Fighting guys, and I
remember one day he also said to me that
the color of my trunks should
match my shin pads. I looked
at him and told him that that
really wasn't what I had in
mind. I didn't want to
wear shin pads, and I only
wanted to wear black. I
will never forget that
because I wasn't in any
position of power, but he
listened to me. I told him
that if I didn't feel right, then I couldn't go
out there and portray my character. Any color
other than black wouldn't give me the feeling I
needed to make it work. And I've worn black
ever since. Wearing black made me feel like I
was that Oakland Raider that I always wanted
to be. I didn't give a shit if I wore the same
color every day, I wanted black.

As for the gloves, they made me look different, and they completed the appearance of the
UFC-style wrestler I wanted to be. Also, I
knew that eventually I was going to have to
punch people in the face. I knew that, in

reality, a punch from a guy my size would open anyone up, so when I progressed to punching people in the face, by wearing the gloves, I'd be protecting my opponent somewhat.

The Spear

Before one of my first matches with Manny Fernandez, Jody Hamilton, the head of the Power Plant, came up to me in the trailer and said, "Whatever you do, kid, do something to start the match off with a bang." I remember it vividly. I didn't tell Manny anything

except that I was going to tackle him. We were circling around, facing each other, and I looked at Manny and said, "Hold on!" and I ran him over.

After the match, I came back to the trailer, and Jody told me, "Kid, whatever you do, *always* use that setup move!" Thank you, Jody.

I had no idea what effect the move would have, but it made perfect sense,

Me spearing the Giant, Paul Wight. And they say wrestling is fake.

since I had been a defensive lineman and tackling was my forte. The fact that the move is called the spear is part of the evolution. It originates from a football term.

Spear n.: A violent tackle using your head as a weapon.

Growing up, my parents told me to use my head, and I guess, in a strange way, I am, although I don't think that this is how they intended me to use it.

The Jackhammer

I was sitting around one night trying to come up with a finishing move, and I thought of a move that combined a suplex and a power slam. I didn't pursue it, though, because I thought it would be too dangerous. A few weeks later, Sarge came up to me and said that he'd been thinking of a finish for me, and he described it. It was the same damn move. Some people think alike. I tried it out at home on my good buddy and human guinea pig, Terry, and then I perfected it on the guys at the Power Plant.

When I first met Dean Malenko, he walked up to me and commented on my finish. "Nice move," he said. "Anytime you want me to teach you how to do it right, let me know." He went on to say, "If you were a real man, you'd do it off the top rope." I just thought he was screwing with me, but I found out later that he used to do a similar move off the top rope when he wrestled in Japan. If I'd known that Dean used it before, in all honesty, I would have changed the move. Never in a million years did I want to copy a move or a spot or anything else, let alone a finishing move, because that is what you're known by. To me it's an unwritten rule that seems to be broken daily: You don't take another guy's finisher. Stealing a guy's finish is like taking food off his plate, and no one will ever be able to convince me otherwise.

Sarge:

We were messing around with some stuff. We got an idea to do something out of a suplex and a corkscrew 'cause originally Bill was doing it where he picked up the guy, did a half little turn with him, and he'd come down like he does now. He learned after doing it a few times that it always can't be a certain way. He got the foundation, then branched out on his own and developed it in his own style. That's how it happened, and now he picks them up straight into the power slam.

The concern for injury eventually took the turn out of the Jackhammer. There was concern, but when Bill sets his mind to do something, he'll do it regardless. I've seen him pick up big Ron Reese, and the Giant—guys you just wouldn't believe.

I had my finishing move, but it needed a name—something powerful, something explosive. I wanted something simple, one word that depicted the move itself and its impact. I was thinking heavy machinery. I thought of the Guillotine and the Piledriver but they had been used before and I wanted something original. Then it came to me. It was actually a name that my father's wife, Arlene, had suggested for my character—Jack Hammer. So, I had a finishing move and it had a name . . . *the Jackhammer!*

Jackhammering the Giant.

Goldberg

The name Goldberg, that's an entirely different story. It came about purely by chance. From the time that I decided to wrestle, I started thinking of names. I was considering calling myself the Beast, or the Annihilator, and I even went so far as considering the name "the Mossad," after the Israeli secret service. The name I liked more than any of them was the Hybrid, which to me described my fighting style. Right before one of my early matches, I remember someone coming up to me and asking me what I wanted to be called, and I said, "Well, I came up with this name, the Hybrid." They performed a copyright search and found the name Hybrid Clothing already registered. There would be a problem with merchandising if they ever did a T-shirt for me, and I thought to myself, *Who cares about that?* I thought, *What the hell, I'll be the Hybrid.* I didn't think that I'd ever have a T-shirt, so I didn't see what the problem was, but thankfully, they saw it differently.

It was my first match in front of a live audience, and as I was headed to the ring, they announced me as Bill Goldberg. I was standing in the middle of the ring, and maybe four people were clapping, and I remember thinking to myself, *I can't believe I actually went through with this. I'm out here in my underwear and calling myself by my real name, and it sure as hell does not sound very menacing.* I thought it was horrible. *Boy,* was I wrong.

Shaquille O'Neal:

Most successful people have a nice ring to their name. Larry Bird . . . Magic Johnson . . . Michael Jordan . . . Gold-*berg!* It's just a nice name, Gold-*berg.* It just sounds mean! That's one of those names, if you're wrestling and you don't know who you're fighting, you hear the announcer say, "Next up—Goldberg," you go, "Goldberg? I'll whip his ass!" But as soon as he comes out, he's one of those guys. He's a specimen! That's what I'm gonna call myself—the Big Goldberg. I like that name!

Pyrotechnics

Most everyone gets generic pyro and the top guys get bangs and a symphony of lights, big to-dos for their entrance. I was asked if I was willing to stand in the middle of the flying sparks. I thought it would look pretty wicked. And most importantly, no one else had ever done it. I try to douse myself with as much water as possible so

that I don't spontaneously combust. But believe me, it's painful. It's something that I can withstand because of its originality and how it sets me off from everyone else. I endure it because of the effect.

The smoke thing was an afterthought. I saw a replay of me standing in the middle of the sparks, and smoke was coming out of my nose and mouth. I asked my dad the doctor if it was hazardous to my health and he told me to check the chemical makeup. It's pure pyrotechnics, which are probably worse than other chemicals, but I only do it once a week. It burns, for sure. It's kind of like sticking a big sparkler up your nose.

At the Palace, Auburn Hills, Goldberg's record is 98-0

TONY SCHIAVONE: *You can't even set the man on fire.*

MEAN GENE OKERLUND: *From the moment he hits that pyro and they crank it up and you see the sparklers and flames and everything go off and he kind of evolves out of it, you can see the GUY HAS GOT STAR WRITTEN ALL OVER HIM. He's a very impressive guy.*

The Theme Music

We were at a Saturday show after my first match, and I went into one of the production trailers, and they were asking me about music for my entrance. Turner has a vast library of different music, and we went through a bunch of different styles before I narrowed it down to a few categories. The technician narrowed it down further, and I really liked this one particular dramatic march. Evidently my music was at one time picked out for Sting. Fortunately, he chose not to use it, because I liked what I heard and went with it.

Gillberg

Since I'm talking about my look, this is a good place to address that Mini-Me-like character that the World Wrestling Federation came up with to make fun of me. When I first heard they were doing a parody of me called Gillberg, I was incensed. I built up this picture in my mind of what it was going to be, and the picture I imagined wasn't nearly as bad as what I eventually saw. I thought it was ridiculous. I wanted to slam everything I saw associated with them and especially the guy doing it, Duane Gill. In retrospect, the guy was just doing his job, but to me, mockery ain't flattery. Even though that guy was getting paid to do it, and it was Vince McMahon's or whoever's idea, I still want to squeeze Gillberg's little head like a grape.

Is that taking the business too seriously? I swore I'd never do that. Oh, well . . .

The Character Goldberg

As a wrestler, I see myself as a cross between Bruiser Brody, Nikita Koloff, Buzz Sawyer, Ken Shamrock, and a wrestling character from one of my favorite movies, *Paradise Alley*—Franky the Thumper. Why these guys? I always admired the relentlessness of Bruiser Brody, the sheer look of Nikita Koloff, the aggressive way of Buzz Sawyer, and the intensity and Shoot Fighting style of Ken Shamrock. As for Franky the Thumper, I just like his character. He was violent, powerful, and a bit scary. By the way, Terry Funk played Franky the Thumper.

chapter five

HUGH'S NEXT

The Saturday-night tapings were done in front of a live audience at Universal Studios. At first, I just did dark matches, which means that they weren't taped, they were just for guys to practice and to get a crowd reaction. Still, wrestling at the tapings was a progression to the next level, which was to perform on TV.

I wrestled various dark matches in Orlando against, among others: Manny Fernandez, Joey Maggs, Bobby Eaton, Hector Guerrero, Sarge, and a couple of the Armstrong brothers. If it weren't for all these guys, I wouldn't be here today. These are the people who got me ready for TV. I'd wrestle them repeatedly, and they were the ones who molded me when I knew absolutely nothing about the profession. A lot of the credit for my success goes to the people who put me over (let me win) in the early days—every one of them. It's important for the fans to know that everyone I wrestled then, no matter how well-known, was invaluable to my experience.

Every match was a learning experience, and I made a lot of mistakes. I dropped Meng and Jimmy Hart on their heads on the same night. They were O.K., but I was upset about it. I've said it many times, I'd rather hurt myself than someone else. In wrestling, you put your life in someone else's hands, and you learn that you have to trust that person whether you like him or not. The business is based on trust. You can be mortal enemies with someone backstage and have your life literally in their hands in the ring. Once you get there, it's all business. It's an unwritten rule that when someone gives you his body, he is giving you his life. You don't take advantage of someone's life.

The Lost Loss

From my first appearance on TV, I won 173 straight matches before suffering my first loss a year and three months later. Although I didn't lose a match during this streak, I did in fact have a blemish on my purported perfect record. And it wasn't against Hector Guerrero, as many people think.

Before my second or third match, we traveled to Dalton, Georgia, to do a dark match at a Saturday-night taping, and Arn Anderson called me into the office and said, "Kid, how do you feel about losing?" I asked him, "Arn, is it real?" and he said no. So I asked him, "Do I get paid any less to lose?" and he said no. "So, who gives a shit?" I said. "It doesn't matter." And I went out and lost. Of course, I really didn't have a choice. They were just testing me to gauge my ego.

Arn Anderson:

I almost swallowed my tongue! Here's this monster who's got as good a look as anybody who's ever walked through a set of ropes. He's just saying, "Sure—I don't mind losing, another day at

My mentor, Arn Anderson.

the park. Pays the same." You don't get that response from the guys in our business these days.

He won me over right away. It was so refreshing to just hear somebody say that. I knew his background, and I deal with a lot of big guys with a lot bigger egos. You can't force your will on them. All you can do is ask, and he made my job very easy that day.

My opponent that night was Chad Fortune, who was a member of Techno Two Thousand when he was with the World Wrestling Federation. I played football against him in the World Football League, when he was a tight end for Frankfurt and I was a defensive tackle for Sacramento. I remember one time he was trying to block me on a swing pass and I was hyped up, cussing and saying something about trying to kill him, and he said, "Hey, watch your language. There are a bunch of Fellowship of Christian Athletes on the field." My reply was short yet sweet: I told him to fuck off. That was our first confrontation, and the second was in the ring.

Ironically, my first loss wound up being to this guy I'd told off on the football field years before, and the only people who knew about it were Chad and the few thousand people watching the match in Dalton.

Monday Night Fever

One night I was sitting around my house, and I got a call from the booking office at WCW, and they informed me that I needed to go to Salt Lake City to be on my first *Monday Nitro.* The show was live on TNT, and I had no idea whom I would be wrestling. I was nervous as shit, and I could barely sleep on the nights leading up to the match. I was given my travel itinerary and boarded the flight early Monday morning. At this point in my career, I was considered extremely green and my extremely green ass was stuffed into a coach seat in the back of the plane. I was in for my first real road trip as a wrestler. When I arrived in Salt Lake City, I picked up my rental car and set out for the arena. I was traveling alone, and I didn't know what to expect. All I knew was that I had to arrive at the arena by 2:00. Unfortunately, the arena that I was headed for was in the opposite direction of the arena where I was supposed to be. So, as I arrived at the wrong place about twenty minutes early, I found only one other person in the parking lot, the Barbarian. And thank god he was there because without him, I never would have found my way to the other arena. So I was late for my first match. I was given the directions on the plane by PeeWee Anderson, the referee, and I think that he was probably goofing with me. That was most likely the first rib of my wrestling career.

I imagined that other wrestlers had heard of me from the Power Plant, and I felt all along that people would be against me. I was the new kid on the block, the outsider, the football player trying to break into their profession. I felt that the other wrestlers kind of compared themselves to me because I was a pro athlete who had played football, who stereotypically would look down on wrestlers and the wrestling business. I don't like to fail at anything, and I especially don't like to have anyone else see me fail. So I was going to work my ass off and make sure that I was going to shove any failure up everyone else's ass. I know that a lot of people in the beginning wanted

A face only a mother could love.

me to fail in some way, shape, or form. If everybody plays his role, then everyone prospers. The fact that I was in that position was just the luck of the draw. The guys whom I knew from before were helping me, which made it a little easier, but in reality, there were still people messing with me daily.

I learned that I would be wrestling Hugh Morrus, A.K.A. Humorous. I didn't know much about Hugh except that he was a seasoned professional. When I met him, it was obvious that he didn't take too kindly to the thought of losing to a guy who was wrestling in his first televised match. I listened to everything he had to say about setting up the match itself. But he had to listen to the booker, and the booker wanted me to win. In wrestling, when you let the other guy win, you're doing a job for him. And Hugh had a job to do. The closer to match time it was, the more nervous I became. To me, first impressions are everything because you can't give them more than once.

September 22, 1997—Salt Lake City

THE PLAYERS:
  Hugh Morrus—6'2", 310 pounds, seasoned veteran from
    Titusville, Florida
  Bill Goldberg—6'3", 290 pounds, unknown newcomer
    from who knows where
  Tony Schiavone—experienced WCW play-by-play guy
  Mike Tenay—wrestling expert and color commentator
  Larry Zbyszko—the Living Legend, former-wrestler-
    turned-bad-guy announcer
  Gene Okerlund—Mean Gene, WCW interviewing legend

(No special entrance for Goldberg, no pyro, no music. Bill Goldberg stands stone-faced in corner with his hands on hips as Morrus enters the ring, climbs through the ropes, and works the crowd.)

TONY SCHIAVONE: *Hugh Morrus will face a newcomer here, Bill Goldberg, a man we know absolutely nothing about, but he is making his debut here, and from the looks of him, he is very determined and looks very powerful.*

(First move—forearm to head—from Goldberg.)

MIKE TENAY: *Tony, I certainly pride myself on knowing the background—the experience factor of the wrestlers involved—but I don't have any information on Bill Goldberg. HELP ME OUT, LARRY!*

TONY SCHIAVONE: *We have stumped Tenay!*

LARRY ZBYSZKO: *FIRE HIM!*

(Morrus dominates match.)

L. Z.: *I don't know much about Bill Goldberg, but we'll just have to watch his movement. Guy looks strong, good shape. He's gonna have to be a man that's got good movement to combat Hugh Morrus.*

T. S.: *Roll-up—nicely done by Goldberg—a submission hold on the leg, and Morrus is going to the ropes.*

M. T.: *Working on the ankle and leg of Hugh Morrus.*

L. Z.: *He's trying to get that figure four on the leg, right there, but he's not in the right ring position. Goldberg, I don't know much about the guy, but just from watching him move, he's gonna have to realize his ring position.*

(Morrus floors Goldberg and goes for his signature finishing move— No Laughing Matter.)

T. S.: *Humorous to the ropes—turnbuckle—going up on the top. HERE'S HIS MOVE. Back flip from the top ropes onto Goldberg. One, two, and—he kicked out.*

L. Z.: *GOLDBERG KICKED OUT!*

T. S.: *HE KICKED OUT!*

M. T.: *THAT'S A SHOCKER!*

L. Z.: *HUGH MORRUS LOOKS SHOCKED!*

T. S.: *You're not kidding, he does! Hugh Morrus with a shocked look on his face. Bill Goldberg kicked out of No Laughing Matter!*

(A back elbow puts Bill on the mat; he gets up and does a back flip!)

T. S.: *How about that back flip? And a power slam!*

M. T.: *And that's a lot to lift—over three hundred pounds of Hugh Morrus!*

T. S.: *And he did it with ease that time! Gonna pick him up again—scoop slam—put him down!*

L. Z.: *HEY—pretty agile for a BIG GOLDBERG!*

T. S.: *To the attack again . . . maybe a vertical suplex?*

(Goldberg raises Morrus over his head as if to suplex him. He almost loses him—the suplex is a little wobbly. He turns him for a power slam. The Jackhammer wasn't named yet.)

T. S.: *Oh, yeah, it is! Combination slam—one-two-three.*

(Goldberg got the pin in 2:42.)

T. S.: *BILL GOLDBERG—OUT OF OBSCURITY—COMES TO NITRO AND PULLS A MAJOR UPSET!!!*

L. Z.: *And Hugh Morrus is not laughing! He got one shot in. . . .*

(Goldberg pulls away from the referee as he tries to raise his hand. Goldberg turns to the camera and says, "That's number one.")

T. S.: *How about that? Not only did he pin him—he kicked out of No Laughing Matter!*

L. Z.: *I think Hugh Morrus got shocked! He gave him his best shot, and Bill Goldberg kicked out of it!*

M. T.: *What a debut for Bill Goldberg!*

T. S.: *INCREDIBLY, with a major upset over Humorous here on* WCW Monday Nitro!

What sticks out about the match is that I kicked out of Hugh's finishing move. I don't think this had ever been done before, and it had to have made him mad. That's when I really started to learn about wrestling. There's a lot of pride in this business, and it was a huge deal that I was the new kid and I came in and kicked out of his finish. In a way, I was taking away from his livelihood, because generally in professional wrestling people don't kick out of other wrestlers' finishing moves. When a wrestler sacrifices his finish to let a nobody get over, it kind of takes them down a notch. A finishing move is supposed to be the end-all. I felt bad about it when we were setting up the match, and I still feel bad when I kick out of somebody's finishing move now. Since Hugh and I have become pretty good friends, Hugh, I'll always owe you one.

I also remember doing a back flip, which was only the third time I had ever done it, and boy, how stupid it was. It was absolutely ridiculous, but I caught people's eyes. I also remember not talking to Gene Okerlund after I exited the ring.

Rick Steiner:

At first, they didn't have him say much. So basically, he was a killing machine, and he fit the mold perfectly.

The legend, Mean Gene Okerlund.

I'm glad that they took this approach, because that's what I would have done if I had control of my character.

L. Z.: *Now, go find out who Bill Goldberg is.*

GENE OKERLUND: *I'm gonna try to find out something about this big man.*

(Okerlund is standing with Bill Goldberg.)

G. O.: *That's very impressive—a gentleman the stature of Hugh Morrus, and you absolutely got in there and manhandled him!*

(B. G. glares and walks away.)

G. O.: *Sir? I've got to get more than that.*

(Goldberg walks up the ramp.)

G. O.: *The gentleman is just walking away from me!*

L. Z.: *IS HE A MUTE?*

G. O.: *I CAN'T BELIEVE THAT! Tony? Larry? I've never seen anything like that! VERY IMPRESSIVE! But who is this guy, Goldberg? You tell me, Tenay!*

M. T.: *NOT A CLUE!*

T. S.: *We don't know, Gene Okerlund, but apparently he is going to talk when he's darn good and ready!*

These are the only things that stick out in my mind about the match. When it was over, I went back to the hotel and stayed up and watched the replay on TV. I woke up the next morning, and it was the first time I ever woke up as a professional wrestler who had been on television. I had fully stepped into those boots, and there was no turning back. As I flew back to Atlanta, I felt like a different person.

The following Monday I flew to Worcester, Massachusetts, for *Nitro,* and I wrestled the Barbarian. This is one of the matches that I will always remember because that's when Eric Bischoff designated Arn Anderson to be my mentor and literally teach me the ropes.

Arn Anderson:

Eric Bischoff came up to me and said, "From this day forward, you are married to Bill. You sit down with him and you go over his matches from *A* to *Z*." I said, "Good! Good! I'll be tickled to death." So I feel like I had a small role in his early success, and that's something that I'll be able to hang my hat on for the rest of my life.

He stuck to me like glue and he taught me everything from then on. He set up all of my matches and worked with me on different spots. He also helped me with character development and promos. Arn is known for having one of the best deliveries in the business, and I attempted to pattern my interviews after his.

Arn Anderson:

The first TV taping they had him come to, I saw Bill. My first impression was *Oh, my god! We've got another one of these monsters that's gonna be impossible to do business with!* Then when I saw what he could do, even at that point being greener than goose shit, I was impressed right away. So, I took an interest in Bill from that day forward.

Even though I had seen very little professional wrestling, I really admired Arn. I thought he was cool. He was the Enforcer, and I used to watch him a bit when I was a kid. He was one of the Four Horsemen. He followed his uncle Ole's footsteps into the ring except in reality, they weren't related and Arn was from Rome, Georgia, not Minnesota, like they said. What an honor it was for me to be just getting started and have one of the best ever as my personal teacher.

I also remember that night in Worcester because I was going to beat the Barbarian, and he was one of the toughest guys out there. By beating him, I was going to be making a huge statement. I was very gracious as usual, and I felt guilty, so I let him do whatever he wanted to me in the ring. This was no big deal because he didn't take advantage of the situation by making himself look good at my expense. But there was one spot where he took me up on the top rope and gave me a belly-to-belly suplex. I had never even climbed on the top rope prior to that, let alone been belly-to-belly suplexed off it. When I went backstage after the match, Eric Bischoff met me and said, "What are you doing, trying to kill me?" "What do you mean?" I asked. He said, "If you're going to let somebody do that to you, *definitely* talk to us beforehand." At the time I wanted to show my willingness to do what the Barbarian wanted me to do. I figured that I owed the veterans something.

T. S.: *Goldberg with a cover one-two and he beat the Barbarian. Bill Goldberg is two and oh—undefeated on* Nitro. *THIS IS NOTHING LESS THAN INCREDIBLE!*

(Goldberg looks at the camera and says, "That's number two!" Then he pushes the camera away.)

T. S.: *Bill Goldberg shocks us for the second straight week. Not only did he win, but he defeated one of the most feared, and powerful, men in our sport!*

(After the match, Okerlund tries to interview Goldberg again.)

G. O.: *I wanted to hold this man up, because in the past week, as Mike Tenay has done, I have done a little research. I don't know if you know who this guy is, but I've got the picture. I know all about him.*

(He pulls a Falcons team picture out of his pocket and shows it to the camera.)

G. O.: *Bill Goldberg, former Georgia Bulldog and Atlanta Falcon. I talked with Rankin Smith himself (the owner of the Falcons), and I know about you, Goldberg! WHY ARE YOU TRYING TO BE A MYSTERY MAN?*

(Goldberg pushes the camera away and walks off.)

G. O.: *HEY, HEY! YOU'RE OUTTA LINE, THERE! YOU ARE OUTTA LINE!*

Gene Okerlund:

That was part of the Goldberg mystique. You saw this phenomenal guy in the ring, and, sometimes, you say more with less in this business. We have guys who "overtalk" it, and that's not the case with Bill Goldberg. He is articulate. He shows tremendous emotion and fire, but he also can do it on a very cerebral plane where things are a little more intellectually thought out as opposed to just a bunch of yelling and screaming. THAT IS NOT GOLDBERG.

In the beginning my matches were really short. It was bing, bang, boom . . . in and out . . . it was easy. I would beat people within two or three minutes, and I wouldn't have to talk. I would wrestle at the beginning of the show, which seemed like an advantage at first, but it turned out to be somewhat of a problem. It was great because I would be done fifteen minutes into the show, and my responsibilities were taken care of, and I could get out of there—I was in and out. After I had done that repeatedly, though, I was advised by a couple of the veterans that the best way for me to learn and become a top-card guy was to watch the top-card guys. Watch the matches up close and ask questions. And to do that, I had to stay throughout the night. Their advice paid off.

Who's Next?

It was about this time that the now well-known Goldberg "battle cry" came into existence. We were doing a Saturday-night taping in San Bernardino on November 1, 1997. I had wrestled in San Diego the night before, and I made the hour-and-a-half drive to San Bernardino with my brother Steve and his good friend Robby Vigilucci. At the arena, we met up with another friend, Roger Duchowny, who had driven down from Lake Arrowhead. Roger has been a movie and TV director for years, and his credits include *The Love Boat, The Girl with Something Extra,* and the hugely successful *The Chimp and I,* which was changed to *Me and the Chimp* when the human demanded top billing over the primate. That's evolution for you.

After the show we found a late-night Mexican restaurant and settled in for some chow and cold *cervezas.* I had known Roger for years, and my new career amused and confused him at the same time. "Billy Goldberg, a wrestler?" he said. "Jews don't wrestle . . . except with guilt." We were all sitting around talking about my new career and listening to Roger's advice. "Always take care of the cameraman," he said. "And you need a catchy phrase, a slogan, something that belongs to you, Billy Goldberg, the wrestler." We talked for hours and somewhere in our animated conversation, we came up with "Who's Next?" although the real credit might go to our waitress, when she was trying to take our order.

I went from Hugh Morrus to the Barbarian to god knows who. I went through guys, and I developed a reputation for beating them with only a couple of moves. I never did an interview for the first eight months. I created intrigue by doing things that people hadn't done before—by providing a simple combination that they hadn't seen. In its infancy, my success, like any wrestler's success, was dictated by the crowd. Many people thought I'd never succeed because I looked like Austin. Although there were some similarities, I felt that my character was unique, and the crowd obviously agreed. I was all business, and my stock was rising.

Of course, the decision to win or lose was out of my hands. The bookers are the ones that come up with the match, and they decide the winner and loser, the story line, and the way it's going to be done. They're the ones that, if necessary, talk the wrestlers into fulfilling their obligation to WCW.

No matter what level you're on, if you understand the business, you and your opponent can have equal input into the planning of the match. This is a very important process, which can be stressful and even confrontational at times.

It doesn't matter who's more popular or who's winning or losing. You're only as good as the guy you beat. If you go out and beat the shit out of a guy in ten seconds, before he throws a punch, that only shows that you can beat him before he gets to you. An adversary that does not dish out some punishment is no adversary at all.

I had to deal with a lot of different personalities in the ring, and I had a hard time with a couple of guys. People can be really tricky. Some guys would make me look like shit because I was green and didn't know how to set up a match. I would win and get to give my finish, but I'd get my ass kicked for what seemed like forty-five minutes. I can honestly tell you that there are many masters of manipulation in the world of wrestling. And I've probably only scratched the surface in finding out who those people are.

Stevie Ray had a problem losing to me on January 5 in Atlanta. I sympathized with him for about five minutes, but then, hey, do what you have to do to make money for the company. The decision is out of your hands. You just have to be a man and do business. It's easy for me to say that, sitting here still being 2,000 to 3. But it's a business, and just like Arn Anderson assured me, it ain't reality. Ever since then, I've treated it like the business that it is. I'm willing to do whatever it takes to be part of the team . . . within reason. My underlying rule is to stay true to the character and always make my performance be as logical as possible.

Nothing should be personal in the ring, and if you take it personally, then you've lost sight of what you're supposed to be doing— entertaining. Although I think a number of people have had a problem losing to me, Stevie Ray is one who really sticks out in my mind. He acted as if I wasn't worthy of beating him. Everyone's entitled to their opinion and I value his, but you have to follow the script.

And I had a problem with Steven Regal that I remember. I think Steve maybe misunderstood what the goal was and took advantage of me in our match by planning moves that would make him look good and me look bad. It was a long match for me. It was grueling, and it made me look pretty bad. I tend to think that no one's doing anything bad to me unless it's blatantly obvious.

Scott Hall and I have had a couple of misunderstandings in the ring, and my opinion of him has been widely publicized, but we'll get to that later. It takes every bit of my professional courtesy to hold back my anger toward him.

The abuse of my inexperience went on until Eric and some of the booking committee stepped in and stopped it. I didn't have a problem with everyone backstage; a couple of guys were actually very helpful, especially Sting. But it certainly wasn't like everybody was jumping to my aid. That's when I realized that if I was going to succeed in this business, I would have to learn through my powers of observation.

Pay-per-view

At my first pay-per-view appearance, I didn't even wrestle. I just had to do a run-in during a match between Alex Wright and Steve McMichael. I didn't have to wrestle during my second pay-per-view appearance, either, because I was supposedly laid out with a lead pipe. My first actual pay-per-view match was for *Starrcade* on

December 28, 1997, in Washington, D.C., just over three months from my first televised match, and I wrestled McMichael. He's a good guy and someone that I idolized when I was growing up. I was a defensive lineman in high school and college; he was one of the top defensive linemen in the NFL (with the Chicago Bears). He was an NFL player who had made the switch to wrestling, which not too many people have done successfully. I knew that I was going to have my share of critics anyway, so the last thing I wanted to do was to try to look like him or copy him in the ring. I didn't want to be stereotyped. I wanted my popularity based solely on my performance and my ability to entertain.

Is this the way to treat an All-Pro like Steve McMichael?

My rivalry with McMichael was inevitable because of our similar backgrounds—we were both football players, we were defensive linemen, and we were big tough guys. Steve taught me a lot in the beginning. Unfortunately, he has been through years and years of pounding from football, much more than I have. But I can sure empathize with him as far as what his body went through. I felt bad when I wrestled him because I was like he was ten years before, all piss and vinegar. Even though wrestling isn't a real situation, I couldn't imagine being in his shoes. We always took great care of each other, and he'll always be a legend in my mind.

I'll Have a Belt, Please

I was in Minneapolis for *Monday Nitro,* and my brother Steve was in town to do some business and firsthand research for this book. He owns three restaurants in the Twin Cities with bald-headed fun-nyman Mikey Andrews. The next day, there was a house show in Mankato, and Mike, Steve, and I took a limo to the match with a couple of other buddies, Dr. Leo and Archie the Punjab. During the show I received a message from Eric Bischoff's secretary, Janey, say-ing that he wanted to meet with me later that night, back in Minneapolis. It was urgent and I was to meet him at the bar in the Ramada Inn near the airport. That night was significant for another reason. It was the first time a fan came up to me and asked me to sign his Goldberg T-shirt.

On the way back to the Twin Cities, I felt compelled to prime myself for the meeting, and Mikey had to pee. We stopped at a bar in Jordan, which is the incest capital of Minnesota, located just out-side of the Valley of the Jolly—ho-ho-ho—Green Giant, in Le Sueur.

Mikey went in first, with Leo close behind. Then Archie, who could have been the first black man ever seen in that bar, followed by the limo driver, who was wearing a big cowboy hat. Steve was next, and I had to go in sideways because of the narrow double-entry doors that were there to keep out the cold and overly large people. Imagine the look on the bartender's face as this parade of characters entered her bar. There was only one person in the place except for the female bartender and he was so drunk that he slid off the stool like a Slinky, like he was a Salvador Dali meltdown. This was a classic small-town bar, replete with pig's knuckles and pickled eggs and all sorts of dried dead meat on the back bar. The drunk guy kept mumbling unintelligibly, and the bartender kept telling him to shut up. Out of nowhere, the guy snapped out of his stupor and recited to the bartender, "Roses are red, violets are blue," I can't remember what he said next but it ended with "f___ you."

When we arrived back in Minneapolis, the limo dropped me off at the Ramada, and I found Eric in the bar, sitting next to Randy "Macho Man" Savage. Although I didn't know why Randy was there at the time, it's quite evident to me now that he was there to help Bischoff sell me on something. We talked for a while, and this was when I first brought up to them how I had been three hours away from signing with the World Wrestling Federation when WCW called. For some reason, the story kind of shocked them!

They were dangling the U.S. belt in front of me like a carrot, and it was a feeling-out process. Basically, Eric wanted to make sure that I was committed to the company, and he wanted to extend my contract in exchange for the opportunity to advance my career. Eric was negotiating with me, and he was a good businessman, no question. That's when I knew that they were going to make a commitment to me, and maybe after the U.S. title, it would be the world title. But they wanted a commitment from me, too. That's when we started to talk about money.

At the time, I was still under my first contract, which gave me a pretty good raise after my first TV match and my first pay-per-view appearance. I remember sitting in Eric's office when I got that first contract, thinking that I'd make a pay raise pretty quickly, but I didn't expect to make it as soon as I did. Little did we know at the time that I'd be on the very next *Monday Nitro* and pay-per-view. I went from my base contract to more than double that amount in less than three weeks. So that's when it started being fun. I started to make some money. From that first pay-per-view on, it didn't matter whether I was at the top of the card or the bottom. I had already surpassed my highest salary with the NFL. That was a milestone for me.

During the meeting in Minneapolis, Eric said that they wanted to offer me a new contract, and that's when I decided to get an agent who was familiar with professional wrestling. I enlisted the services of Barry Bloom and Michael Braverman. Barry and Michael were very reputable, and they represented a very select group of top guys. Kevin Nash and Scott Hall introduced me to them, and they supposedly weren't accepting any new clients at the time. But they made an exception with me. You hear that "not accepting new clients" line a lot from agents, but in reality, they'll make exceptions for anyone that will make them enough money. I love those guys, but that's the way it is, and I understand that. I'd do the same thing if I were in their shoes. So I signed with them, and it was a totally different story this time around. After a lot of negotiation, I worked out a new contract, and I stepped up to a different level once that contract was signed—a level which was pretty cool for me.

The match with Raven was set for April 20, in Colorado Springs. It would be two Jews grappling for the U.S. title, Bill Goldberg versus Scott Levy, and I was really excited to get the title shot. I had met Raven in passing at various rock-and-roll clubs in Atlanta before I was a wrestler. He was a very good worker who could make a guy look great. What more could I ask for? I had a title shot; I was going over; I got to bounce my opponent all over the ring; and he was going to make me look great in the process.

(Goldberg is 74–0 at this point. Legendary ring announcer Michael "Let's Get Ready to Rumble" Buffer introduces Goldberg: "hometown—unknown; weight—unknown." The match is being held under Raven's rules, which means that there aren't any.)

L. Z.: *He moved the Rocky Mountains with a single arm; he punched out Pikes Peak, and he leaped over Colorado Springs in a single bound. If Raven doesn't have kryptonite, he better fly the coop.*

(Raven lays the belt on the mat. He and Goldberg stare each other down, then Raven charges at Goldberg.)

T. S.: *The one undeniable fact about Goldberg is the power!*

(Raven grabs a chair on the outside and hits Goldberg in the gut and on his back. He pounds on Goldberg in the corner.)

M. T.: *The pain is registering, but it has no effect on Goldberg.*

(Goldberg spears Raven, prompting Raven's buddies, the Flock, to attack. Goldberg throws Billy Kidman out of the ring. Horace Hogan hits Goldberg with stop sign. Reese lifts Goldberg up—Goldberg head-butts him.)

T. S.: *Oh, my god! He's gonna try to pick him up!*

(Goldberg somehow hits the Jackhammer on Reese, sending a tremor throughout the ring and the arena.)

L. Z.: *That's a ten on the Richter.*

T. S.: *WOW—that man is almost five hundred pounds. What a show of strength by Goldberg!*

That was the first time I'd jackhammered Reese on TV, and I almost gave Bischoff a heart attack when I did it because it wasn't part of the gig. What he didn't know was that Reese was the guy I perfected my Jackhammer on at the Power Plant. He was six foot ten and four hundred pounds. I had been taught by Sarge and by everyone else in the embryonic stage of my career that if you can't do your finish to everyone, then there's no point in doing it. It was important to me to be able to do the move on everybody. He was the biggest guy available, so I practiced on him.

Then I took the stop sign from Horace Hogan—Hulk's nephew—speared Raven, and won the belt.

M. T.: *The fans stopped him and threw him over the guardrail. They're here to support Goldberg in any way they can!*

(Goldberg spears Raven.)

T. S.: *Everyone is standing! As Goldberg is going for it—right now!*

(Goldberg hits the Jackhammer, gets the pin, and the crowd roars.)

L. Z.: *We've got a new champion, and Goldberg is open for business.*

T. S.: *GIVE THAT MAN THE BELT. Goldberg is the United States Heavyweight Champion, and he won it in grand style!*

(Goldberg to the camera, "IT'S MINE!")

M. T.: *Chalk up victory number seventy-five in a row.*

L. Z.: *Seventy-five and zero!*

T. S.: *Seventy-five and oh! He fought off every member of the Flock. GOLDBERG FEARS NO MAN. HE'S THE CHAMPION—live, on* Monday Nitro!

L. Z.: *Congratulations to a man who's worked harder than anybody I've seen.*

T. S.: *WHAT A MOMENT! GOLDBERG IS THE CHAMP!*

Me.

Raven.

Sting:

Bill does this deal where he jumps up in the air and looks into the camera, and he grabs the top ropes and his traps are sticking up above his head and he does the yell, or the scream, and his eyes are on fire. Man, I mean that's FIRE! CHARISMA! When what you do is believable and it looks like you're murdering people and then you jump up and do that, people are gonna just eat it up, and they did!

A lot had happened in the short time that I had been a professional wrestler. It was a year and seven months since I signed my first contract, a year and two months since I started at the Power Plant, and seven months since my first TV match. I was seventy-five and zero (except for the lost loss), and life was good. My life began to change when people started to notice me. It was harder and harder to have free time, but along with a few disadvantages came more opportunities. I was asked to participate in more charities and do more worthwhile work so that people could benefit from what I had accomplished. Which in itself is pretty strange because I didn't invent a cure for cancer; I was just in the right place at the right time. I was living the American dream!

chapter six

THE UNITED STATES AND THEN THE WORLD

As much as I'd talked about not putting a lot of emphasis on having a belt, when I beat Raven it was kind of cool. I have always understood that my being a champion was just part of the show. Still, since I was bestowed with the honor of being chosen to wear the belt, I was going to take pride in it. And it was my responsibility to carry it all over the country to my matches. This presented a bit of a problem getting through airport security sites. It's hard to explain a professional wrestling championship belt to a Ugandan security guard.

When I first started out on the road, I traveled alone. After a few months I ran into Kevin Nash and Scott Hall after a flight to Philly or somewhere, and they just asked me if I wanted to jump in and ride with them. It became a regular occurrence for a while, and they smartened me up a lot about

U.S. Champ, Goldberg.

the business. Now I'm always worried about what, if any, ulterior motives someone might have. That's what this business does to you. Anyway, I was appreciative of those guys showing me the ropes and I traveled with them for a while. When Scott would take his periodic trips to rehab, I still sometimes traveled with Kevin. As you can imagine, Kevin and I became friends, considering the number of times that Scott was in and out of the clink.

When I traveled with Kevin and Scott, Kevin never did anything to turn me off him as a person. But Scott, just in the way he carried himself, I never thought he was a good representative for the business. I didn't like the way he treated people. He was arrogant and rude. The fact that he was a heel at the time just gave him an excuse to be a dick.

Kev's a good guy, you just have to understand that he stirs up a lot of shit. He's a master manipulator. But, you know, I think he's business. Big Kev has helped me quite a few times, so for that I'm appreciative. There's nothing that Scott Hall could ever do to change my opinion of him. Not a damn thing. Being drunk is no excuse for being a jackoff. The way he handles himself in public is despicable, and I'm not alone in my opinion of him. He has heat with the majority of the planet. He should crawl back to everyone at WCW and beg for his or her forgiveness. Do you think I like him? I could write an entire book about how I feel about Scott Hall. But I suppose there are jerks in any business, and wrestling is no exception. The way a couple of people deal with the public is embarrassing, and sometimes I try to overcompensate for their actions. As a whole, there are some great guys here. They just don't stick out as much as the pricks.

Curt Hennig and I became pretty good friends. When you're on the road as much as we are, you have to keep yourself amused, and Curt Hennig may be the king of the practical jokers. Curt is from the Minnesota wrestling contingent, and his father—Larry the Ax—was one of the best wrestlers ever. I've learned a lot from both

Larry and Curt, and I don't think that Curt gets the credit he truly deserves.

Larry the Ax is well respected in the world of professional wrestling and he paid me one of the highest wrestling compliments that I could have ever received. On April 19, 1998, my brother Steve and our good friend Mike Andrews and I were the guests on the *Dark Star* radio show in Minneapolis. Larry the Ax called in and said, "Bill, you should be very proud of yourself for what you've done in wrestling." He went on to say that he was proud of me for representing the new generation of wrestlers. It really meant a lot to me, coming from such a no-B.S. guy. To me, that was like getting an endorsement from the Pope, if I weren't Jewish.

Curt used to play tricks on people all the time and there are a number of things that I'd love to tell you but he'd probably get a couple of guys after me if I did. Once we were taking a flight together and I was the last one on the plane, and evidently Curt told everyone around us in first class that I'd been sick and had the runs. I got up and went to the bathroom and he turned around and told everyone "See, I told you" and he secretly sprayed this nasty, disgusting poop spray near my seat. When I came back, it really stunk and I was laughing because I knew Curt had used the spray. But what I didn't know was that the joke was on me because everyone in first class was laughing too, thinking I'd had an accident. Hennig does that stuff all the time.

Traveling Man

Life on the road really sucks. It's something I'm not used to and something I never want to get used to. When I played in the NFL, when I actually traveled with the team, we traveled about nine times a year. Now I can travel nine times in nine days. But the truth is, I don't have it nearly as bad as some people. I've heard of guys being on the road for twenty-five straight days. I couldn't imagine that. I think I was on the road for sixteen or seventeen once. There've been guys who have been on the road for most of their lives. It sucks being away from home, away from my girlfriend, my animals, and my friends.

You fly into a town, you rush to work out, you rush to eat, and you have to be at the arena about six hours before you go live. You get to the building, you go through all the stress, and you leave tired and sore. You jump in your car, and if the next venue is less than three hundred miles away, you have to drive it, either that night or the next morning. Look at Kevin, he's seven feet tall and his knees must kill him when he drives. Sometimes you're behind the wheel for hours after your match and you can't find anywhere decent to eat. Typically, I don't hit the road until close to 11 P.M., and I haven't eaten since 5:30. I end up eating fast food or in some brightly lit all-night restaurant. Eventually, I settle in at the hotel. I sleep in a different hotel almost every night. It would make it a lot easier if I could stay in the same place for more than one night, but logistically that rarely works. Bummer.

THE WORST PARTS OF BEING ON THE ROAD

Eating in crappy restaurants

Trying to find a good gym

Getting beat up day after day, physically and mentally

Not sleeping in your own bed

Not sleeping in the same bed more than one night

Driving from town to town

Missing my girlfriend and my animals

Simple things make a big difference on the road. Like having pillows that don't feel like they're stuffed with bricks. A good, firm mattress and functional air-conditioning. Some towns are so small that they don't have a decent gym, so the only place to work out is the local YMCA. The weather can also be a problem; driving through snow and sleet is commonplace. Hell, I feel like a postman. A postman who's been thrown around the ring, that is. I eat, sleep, drive, work out, and try to keep sane. At times, I enjoy traveling alone because I'm too drained to talk. Any bit of serenity helps.

As you can imagine, the wrestling life can take its toll, and a lot of guys have passed away since I started out. This business has swallowed up a lot of people, like Rick Rude, Louis Spicoli, Rick "Renegade" Williams, and Bobby Duncum, Jr., just to name a few. But it's just like anything else—if you're not careful, you can become a victim of your environment. They showed me what can happen if you don't take care of yourself. They just ran a bit hard. It's a shame what the business can do to some people.

THE BEST PARTS OF BEING ON THE ROAD

Driving through beautiful parts of the country

Having peaceful and quiet drives

Escaping the constant ringing of my telephone (no one knows where I am)

Getting to go to some very good restaurants

How do I keep my sanity in this business, and being on the road all the time? I have yet to figure that out. I try to stay by myself, to get a routine down, and to stick to it as much as possible. You can try to have a positive attitude, but when one bad thing happens on the road, it seems to snowball.

The Chant

It was June 1, 1998, and I was in D.C. for *Monday Nitro*. It was during the hockey playoffs. I love hockey, it's such a violent sport. Any sport that you can beat the shit out of somebody and just sit in a penalty box for two minutes is O.K. by me. I was standing backstage and my music started up and the crowd started chanting, "Goooooold berrrrrg, Goooooold berrrrrg," and to me it sounded like a hockey chant. The hair on my arms stood up on end and the adrenaline was flowing. I thought, *Man, this is the coolest shit in the world*. It was awesome. I was never in wrestling to get that response,

but I suppose something that I was doing was working. When I first heard that chant and felt that sensation, I knew what people were talking about when they tried to explain that feeling, that chill you get. I had all of those people chanting for me, and of all types of chants, a hockey chant. There you go . . . I was having fun.

I heard what I thought was a vicious rumor that the chant was being piped in. After questioning members of our production staff, I found out that the rumor was, in fact, true. At times, the chant was prerecorded. This embarrassed me to no end, and it stopped soon after. I thought it was ridiculous. I'll obviously go to certain lengths to set the stage for a choreographed event, but a fake chant is going a bit overboard for me.

The Ring Leaders

The more I wrestled, the more I learned, and I quickly discovered the importance of the referee. The ref is like a field general in the ring. He points you in the right direction, he tells you how much time is left in the match, he tells you if you're going to commercial, and he'll relay an important message from one wrestler to another—like, "Where are you going for a beer after the match?"

The referees have to be good actors to pretend to control a match that has rules that are meaningless. These guys are also a different breed. They may be the brunt of a lot of our jokes; but the point is, we couldn't do what we do without them. A lot of them were amateur wrestlers, and some come from wrestling-ref families. One example is Brian Hildebrand. He was a classic ref, and a great guy. He had an amateur wrestling background and he enjoyed many years of wrestling all across the world. Unfortunately for all of Brian's friends and family, he had terminal cancer. He was working almost up to the day he died. We all miss him.

A referee can screw up a match, too. He can make you look like a fool. He can be in the wrong place at the wrong time. He can actually be watching when you come in the ring with a chair that he's not supposed to see. That moment when he sees you means the match should be a disqualification, and when it isn't, it makes you look bad and it makes him look bad.

Mickie Jay, Nick Patrick, Billy Silverman, and Charles Robinson are very good guys and very good referees. In reality, the refs, the camera guys, and the guys in the trucks should be your best friends. They're all instrumental in the success of the match. I goof on the refs all the time. You've got to keep them on their toes.

The Toughest and Strongest Wrestlers

Shortly after I started to wrestle, I became friends with Meng and the Steiners. Those guys are so strong, they could pick up a building. Scott Norton is a former national arm-wrestling champion who may even be stronger than those guys. He's benched well over six hundred pounds, which is amazing. Then there's Bryan Adams, A.K.A. Crush, who's also very impressive. Luger is another guy who's strong in the gym.

Obviously, Paul Wight, A.K.A. the Giant, A.K.A. the Big Show, is a monster. One day I was sitting at the dinner table in San Bernardino, passing time before a house show. Paul came up behind me and pushed down on my shoulders until the folding chair I was sitting on collapsed. At seven feet, 540 pounds, Paul is a man monster, and with little effort he made the tubular steel chair collapse like an accordion. He just started laughing, and walked away down the hall, puffing on the ever-present cigarette that was dangling from his lips. From my new seat on the floor I flung the flattened chair down the hall after him, and he nonchalantly sidestepped it. One of the bookers at the time, Kevin Sullivan, was sitting at the end of the hallway casually eating his dinner when the chair took out two of the legs of his table. It was like slow motion when his dinner slid down the slanted table onto the floor. The Giant just sneered at Kevin and kept on walking.

In terms of brute strength, Fit Finlay and Sarge are right up there pound for pound. Chris Benoit is tough, and Rey Mysterio, Jr., takes a beating the way he flies around in and out of the ring. Tank Abbott also should be mentioned because of his involvement in No Holds Barred competition. But without a doubt, Meng and the Barbarian are the pinnacles of natural strength and toughness.

I respect certain guys in this business for being realistic and being tough but not going out there and killing people like they could. Robbie Rechsteiner, A.K.A. Rick Steiner, is at the top of that list, along with his brother, Scott. Robbie's just a genuine guy. He's a country boy who likes to hunt and fish. He's a good family man, and he's stuck by me through thick and thin. He's always been there for me. He's objective in what he tells me and he just gives me good advice. He sticks up for me, and he tells me when I'm right and wrong, and he has no ulterior motives. And that's so hard to find. He's just a friend, and I appreciate the hell out of that. I'd do any-thing for him. Man, I really would. And there aren't many people I'd say that about. He's a great guy. The fact is, though, he and his brother are nothing less than lethal. They both are suplexing machines who revel in the fact that they could destroy just about everything in their paths, both in and out of the ring.

Sting

After winning the U.S. title, my first big match was on June 13, when I had the honor of wrestling my buddy Sting. Wrestling Sting, the guy I revered more than anyone from the beginning, was like a dream. For me, it was like wrestling Hogan, because wrestling those guys meant I'd made it, in a sense. It was also extremely weird. It was weird because he got me into the business and I've always looked at him like he was the king of WCW, and I never envisioned myself rising to that level. When I started wrestling, I used to joke, "Well, I'll get in there and wrestle Sting after a few weeks." When I finally did wrestle him, it was great, because I enjoyed watching him and I knew the combination could make for a great match. Every time we wrestle, we try to put something special into it, to do something new. It's an honor wrestling against him or with him. Wrestling with him is special because he's the fan favorite and you get a different kind of feeling, a kind of warmth from the crowd. But wrestling against him was still exciting, because I knew it would be worthwhile to watch. Being in there with Sting was the next step up the ladder of success.

Helping out my friend Sting.

Here I am trying to figure out where to throw
my good friend Rick Steiner.

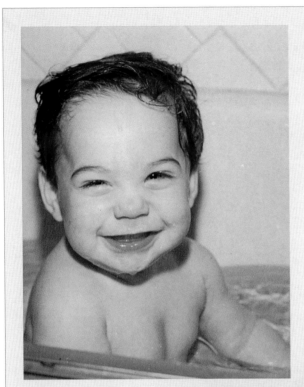

Baby Goldberg.

Hanging out with my
grandmother, Rene.

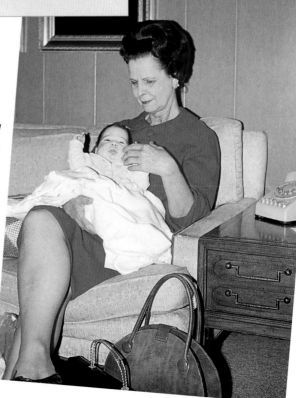

Writing my name in
the ocean.

Me, my mom, and
my leisure suit.

With my mom and
dad on my first day
at Georgia.

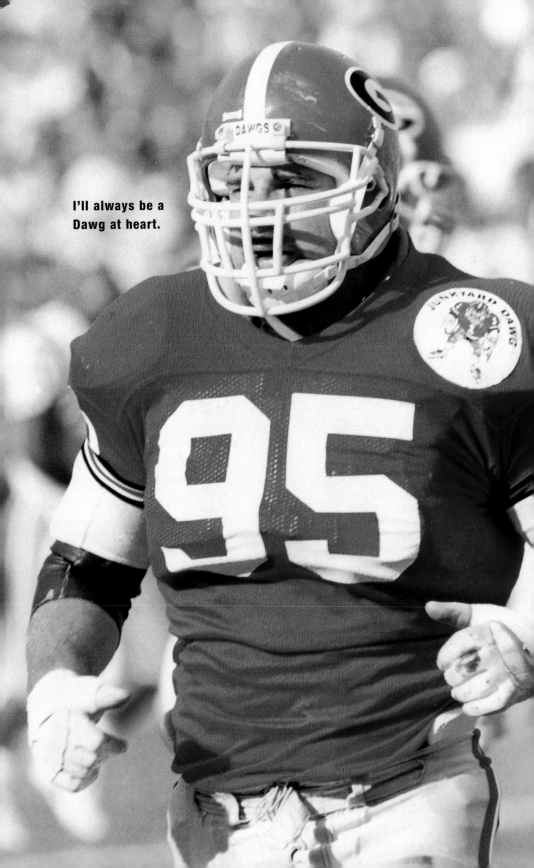

I'll always be a Dawg at heart.

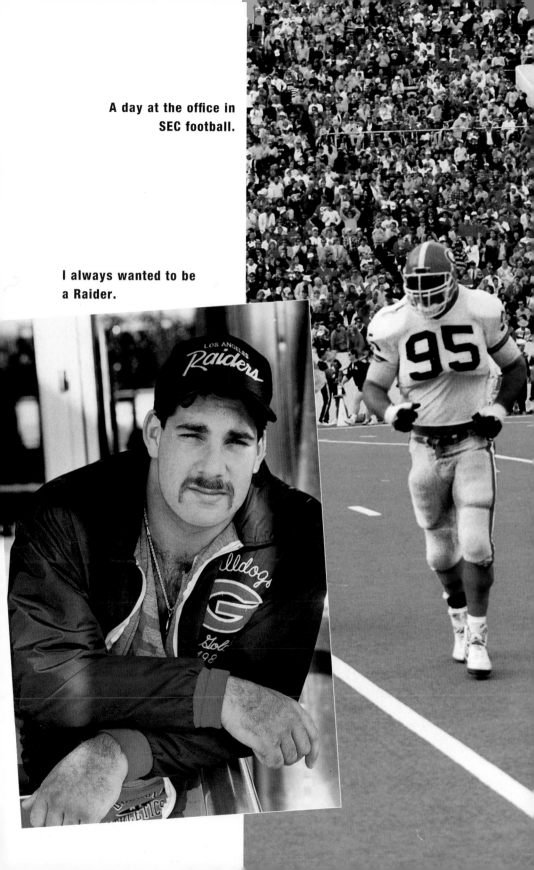

A day at the office in SEC football.

I always wanted to be a Raider.

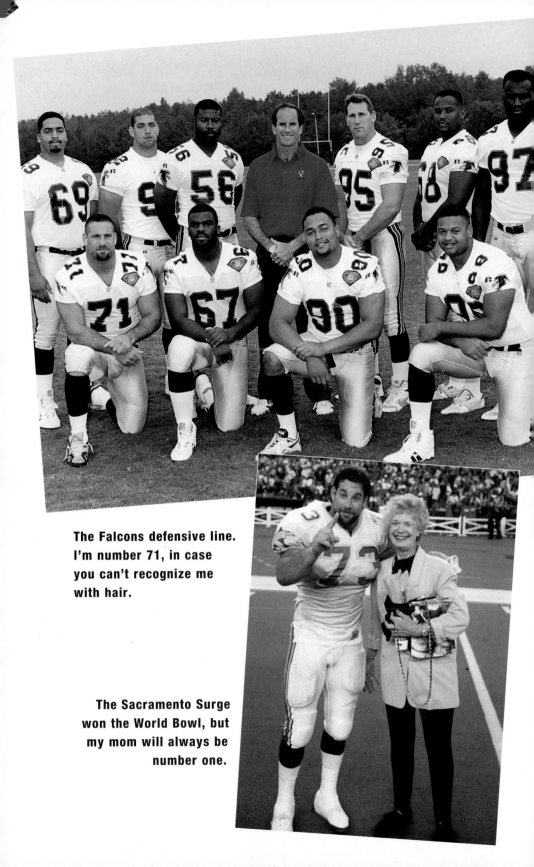

The Falcons defensive line.
I'm number 71, in case
you can't recognize me
with hair.

The Sacramento Surge
won the World Bowl, but
my mom will always be
number one.

Don't try this at home.

Sid Vicious is a scary sight at Halloween Havoc.

Winning a test of strength with the legendary Hulk "Hollywood" Hogan.

High flying.

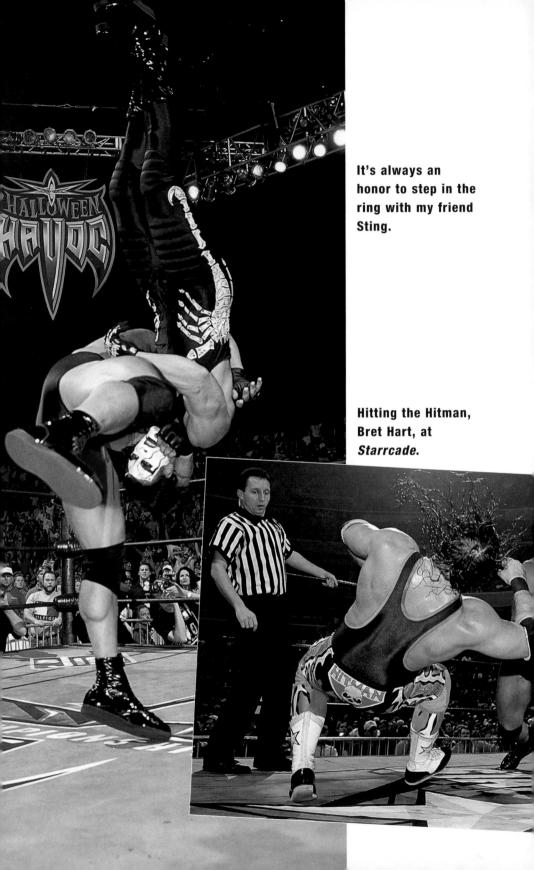

It's always an honor to step in the ring with my friend Sting.

Hitting the Hitman, Bret Hart, at *Starrcade*.

Surfing with Steve, Brad Stagg, and Harvey Williams.

**Me, my buddy Scott Adams, and some big halibut on
an NFL alumni fishing trip.**

At home in Atlanta with my girlfriend, Lisa, and my dogs.

Hanging with my buddies Ted Berkowitz, Larry Brown,
and Terry Shields at the Firecracker 400.

Here I am with
Cincinnati Reds pitcher
(and Goldberg fan)
Danny Graves.

One of the best players
in baseball, Ken Griffey, Jr.

Batting practice with Mark McGwire
and my old friend Ron Gant.

Me, NASCAR great Bill Elliot, and Lisa.

With Charles Barkley backstage at a show.

Me and the Gov, Jesse Ventura.

"Who Am I"
Who am I? I am courage.
Who am I? I am determination.
Who am I? I am the guy who gets knocked down, but always gets
back up.
Who am I? I am the guy who won't quit until my good
is better
than best..

Now I ask, "Who are you?"

Written by
Chad Dunn

I knew Chad Dunn for three years and he was one of my best friends. He was an incredible human being and I miss him a lot.

My best buddy, Barron.

The World Is Mine

My biggest match ever was against Hollywood Hogan for the World
title. It was supposed to be a dark match on *Nitro,* to get people to
go to the Georgia Dome. I was still undefeated, and I was real nervous because I was wrestling Hogan—win, lose, or draw, it was
Hogan. The guy who made wrestling a household name. If it weren't
for him, I wouldn't have had the opportunities that I've had. He
paved the way for guys like me to go mainstream and be taken a little more seriously. I learned a lot about the business by talking to

Here's mud in your eye.

him and by watching him. Watching how he deals with people, watching how he deals with wrestlers, watching how he deals with the crowd. Now I was going to watch him from inside the ring!

I was sitting with my buddy Terry in my living room watching *Thunder* the Thursday before the dark match, and J. J. Dillon came out and said that he had an important announcement to make. "We're going to have a title match Monday night, and it's going to be Hollywood Hogan against Goldberg," he announced. I was surprised, to say the least. My first thought was *O.K., thanks for telling me, guys, I see how this is going to be.* There's nothing like being prepared, so I flipped out from the time I heard the announcement to the time I showed up at the Georgia Dome on Monday. I was nervous being in my home state where I played football and went to school, and I'm sure there were a lot of people there wanting to see how ridiculous I was going to look. They wanted me to fail; at least, in my mind, they did. In my life, I've probably tried harder not to fail than I've tried to succeed. In wrestling, I wanted to prove everyone wrong, instead of proving myself right. I wanted to be able to say, "I told you so."

I showed up for the match and Hogan attempted to calm me down. He told me to relax and leave it all up to him. What an honor to be in the ring with the man who made wrestling what it is today. There was a stipulation that in order to face Hogan, I first had to beat Scott Hall. Scott and I concentrated on trying to have a good match. But Scott is Scott, and sometimes it's difficult to communicate with him. Unfortunately, we got to a certain point in the match and I got lost. I just went blank. He was lying on his back, and he accused me of not wanting to run the spot. That's not what happened—I just totally forgot it. I was young and green and it was unfortunate. But anyway, somehow we finished the match. I beat

On top of the world in Atlanta.

him, and I was tired—exhausted physically and mentally. But this was only the beginning.

There were 41,000 in the arena, and I was more than excited. I remember Hogan saying, "Just follow me out there, kid." As I heard Michael Buffer, the most recognizable voice in ring sports today, I got chills up and down my spine. I was nervous as shit. The next thing I knew, I was walking to the ring in awe of my surroundings. It was surreal. We locked up, and people went crazy. It was like the Super Bowl, and everyone was cheering for me because I had home-field advantage. Halfway through the match, he put me in a front face-lock. That's not usually a lethal move—unless your opponent is covered in Icy Hot. It got all over my face and my eyes, and I could barely see for the rest of the match. It burnt the hell out of my eyes. If you watch the tape you can tell something was wrong.

In the end, I was very hesitant to spear Hogan because I didn't want to hurt him. My motto when I'm wrestling is to make things look realistic but to keep the other guys safe at all times. With Hogan, it felt like I had my whole career in my hands. I was a little more careful with him than with anyone else. In the end, I jack-hammered him and got the pin. I was handed the belt, and I raised both of those belts up. Man, that was awesome—it was the best moment in my wrestling career, for sure, if not my life. It was pretty damn cool, and I can't compare it to anything. That feeling is one of the things that keeps me going. On July 6, 1998, I became the WCW Heavyweight Champion of the World!

chapter seven

WHAT GOES UP MUST COME DOWN

Beating Hogan gave me a lot more credibility and I began wrestling the top guys in the WCW. I wrestled Scott Hall again, then Curt Hennig, and my next big match was at the *Road Wild* pay-per-view in Sturgis, South Dakota, on August 8. I wrestled in a Battle Royal, and it was one of the battle royalest screwups of all time. In the ring, it was me, the Giant, Scott Hall, Curt Hennig, Konnan, Lex Luger, Kevin Nash, Scott Norton, and Sting.

At the end, everyone was eliminated except the Giant and me. The finish of the match was not what was supposed to happen originally. I wasn't supposed to beat the Giant that night. There were differing opinions about the finish of the match. Not between the Giant and me, but between others backstage. We weren't supposed to have

Face to chest with the Giant.

93

a deciding match until the year's biggest pay-per-view, at *Starrcade* in December, and it was only August. It should have been built up for a larger match than that Sturgis pay-per-view, for sure. I think the company lost a big opportunity that night, and we screwed ourselves out of the big payday. That match was the beginning of the end for a Goldberg-Giant rivalry.

Goldberg, Greenberg—They're Not the Same

Before he was Y2J in the World Wrestling Federation, Chris Jericho was a cruiserweight trying to make a name for himself in the WCW. One of the ways he did this was by trying to pimp me. He'd talk about me in his promos. He even went so far as to promise a match against me at the *Fall Brawl* pay-per-view. Only, when it was time for me to make my entrance, it was a four-foot-tall version of me that came through the curtain in  my place. I was at home recovering from knee surgery. Of course, Jericho squashed the guy in about two minutes, and then went around talking about how he'd stopped my streak. Then he took the insult a step further by calling me "Greenberg" in his promos.

I had about one sentence to say to Jericho when I made my return. I looked at him as seriously as I could, and I said, "I hope it was worth it." That was one of the first times that I took this business too seriously. I didn't like Jericho's whole gimmick, and I didn't want to be a part of it, because I thought it was embarrassing. That was the comedy aspect of wrestling that I wanted to stay away from. But in reality, the idea of him coming after me was so stupid that it got him more over as a heel. At the time, I thought it made me look bad. But it turned out to be another learning experience for me. It served a purpose, and I was pissed off at the company for letting him do it—but who knows, maybe it was entertaining.

DDP

Dallas Page helped me out a lot in the beginning of my career. He did a lot to try to get me into the business. I appreciate all of his help. Dallas gets a little goofy at times, no question. He seemingly has his own agenda, but he also can be very giving at times. You just have to ground him. You have to try and keep Page Falkenberg from being Dallas, but they're really the same person. I've learned how to deal with Dallas.

We always have good matches. Dallas has a fast pace, and he's a different kind of worker. He'll run round a lot and bounce off of you, and he'll use his cunning ways to get what he wants. He knows what he's doing, and he's a good character. But Dallas does it Dallas's way, and you learn to deal with that. Every time we have a match it's entertaining.

My match with Dallas at *Halloween Havoc* on October 25 was one of the best matches I've ever had. He is very meticulous in his planning, and you're always in for a long night's work when you wrestle him. I learned a lot from that match—about myself, and about the business. We took pride in the fact that we had a good match. I entrusted him with a lot that night, and he came through for me. Toward the end of the match, I went to spear him, and he left a little bit early for some reason. I ended up spearing my head into the mat, like a lawn dart. Basically, I knocked myself out. I rolled over, shook out the cobwebs, and finished the match. That was the hardest obstacle I ever had to overcome during a match—and to be honest with you, I don't remember the end of it. It looked pretty devastating. The way I see it, as long as it doesn't cause permanent damage, it makes for a good show.

They played the match again the following night on *Nitro* because the pay-per-view went over the time limit and thousands of viewers missed the match. Rather than refund their money, they decided to show the match on free TV. At the time, it was the highest-rated TV match in wrestling history.

Diamond Dallas Page and I always have good matches.

Okla-homecoming

I went back to Tulsa for the first time as a wrestler on December 18, 1998. It was my homecoming, and they even presented me with the key to the city. The lady who introduced me even had the nerve to call me Billy. I wrestled the Giant in the main event. We wanted to put on a good show, but no more than a minute and a half into the match, he threw me into the turnbuckle and I sliced my head on the ringpost. Unfortunately, I hit an artery and ended up spraying a couple of my friends in the second and third rows with blood.

I knew I was bleeding pretty badly, so I prepared to end the match with a spear. But the ref didn't see it that way. He wanted us to finish immediately because he saw that I was losing consciousness. I still wanted to jackhammer him, but that was biting off more than I could chew. I body slammed him and it was one, two, three, and I was off to the hospital. Next thing I knew, I was sitting in the hospital room and everything was fine. Except for my oldest brother, Mike, was there taking pictures of my wound and the doctors sewing it up. And people want to know where I get my sick sense of humor from. Go figure.

Not the first and certainly not the last.

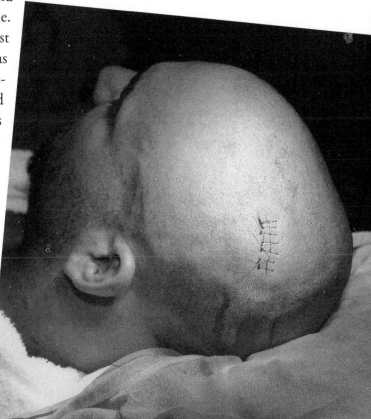

Some Guys I'd Love to Wrestle
in That Other Federation

I watch the World Wrestling Federation programming every once in a while, and I watched quite a bit when I was out hurt. I have the utmost respect for a lot of their guys. Obviously, I'd love to wrestle Steve Austin. I think there'd be no other opponent out there who would be more intriguing for my character, considering our similarities. I met him at a licensing show in New York, but I don't know him very well as a person. I've spoken to him a couple of times, and I very much respect what he does, no question. He's made it to a level that is almost unparalleled. Unfortunately, Austin's limited because of his knee and neck injuries. So future battle plans for the two of us may never become a reality.

The Rock would be another obvious choice, based upon his popularity and how exciting he is in the ring. There's no question that he's a good representative for the business. I'd love nothing more than to have a match with the Rock and Austin. Hell, I'd like to wrestle both at the same time, make it a handicap match. I'll love the Rock to the day I die for the time he called and offered to help my mother when a hurricane was approaching Miami. We finally met when I was with Wayne Gretzky at a Maple Leafs game the night before Gretzky was inducted into the Hockey Hall of Fame.

The Rock is a football player. Man, he's six foot five, 270 pounds, and I admire what he can do. He can fly around like anybody. And so can I. We have something that separates us from a lot of people. It's called explosive speed.

I met Mick Foley at Main Event Fitness years ago, before I started wrestling. He seems like a great guy. I respect him because he always wanted to be a big-time wrestler and he attained that goal. He even won the World Championship. The only problem that I have is that he had to sacrifice his body to meet his goal—and to me, that's not worth it.

Foley can take a beating. But it's hard to respect him for that alone. I respect his passion for the game, but I think he's crazy for doing the things that he's done. But, like I said, that's just my opinion, and I don't ever want to talk badly about him, because he's a great guy. It's just a shame that his body is suffering. He's going to be hobbling around like the old Raider, Jim Otto, after umpteen knee surgeries, and that sucks. He reminds me of Nick Nolte in *North Dallas Forty.*

Then there's Hunter Hearst Helmsley. I've heard that he's said some derogatory things about me. Whether he has or not, when I met him, he was a cocky prick. I'd love to turn heel on his ass in the ring any day.

Why Is This Night Different Than All Other Nights

It was December 27, 1998, the worst birthday of my life. I was going to lose my match and the Heavyweight belt to Kevin Nash, at the *Starrcade* pay-per-view in Washington, D.C. Needless to say, it seemed quite strange to me that just a week or two after he obtained the job of booker, Kevin became the guy that "finally" beat me. I sustained my first loss at the hands of him and Scott Hall.

Something's up.

I remember that I was uncomfortable with the whole thing at the time. I tried not to read anything into it, but it was hard not to. I showed up, I did my job, I listened to fifteen hundred or so people give their opinions, but, ultimately, I listened to my boss, Eric Bischoff. Even though I thought that Eric was being swayed by a number of people, my responsibility is to do what my boss tells me to do. So I went out there, got zapped by Scott Hall, powerbombed by Nash, and lost the match.

After you ride a roller coaster that's only going up for a year and a half, and you reach the pinnacle and then dive straight down with no gradual decline, it's a little disorienting. At that point, I didn't know how to take losing. It was something that was foreign to me, but realistically, it was a work. Because I lost didn't mean I'd done anything wrong, it was just meant to be part of the entertainment. It was only hard to handle because I know that there were people backstage trying to undermine my success for one reason or another. I didn't have any problem with actually going out and doing my job. The next night on *Nitro,* Hogan poked Nash in the chest with his finger, Nash took a dive, and Hogan walked off with the belt.

The next pay-per-view didn't go much better for me. On January 17, at *Souled Out* in Charlestown, West Virginia, I wrestled my good friend Scott Hall in a tazer/ladder match. I had never done a ladder match before, and I had a bad knee, but because the show had been advertised, we went through with the match. I was injured and inexperienced, and therefore it was one of the worst matches I think I've ever been involved in. I still don't understand why, in a business that is choreographed like ours, steps can't be taken to alter the match or give the crowd something else instead of what they're promised when one of the wrestlers is injured like I was that night. To me, a guy's health is more important than one pay-per-view match. Still, I always enjoy beating Scott Hall.

Flair Out

Ric Flair has been a legendary wrestler for a long time. He's done a lot of good for this business, and he's done nothing but help me. He's also been a family friend for many years. A couple of months ago when he won the World Title belt for the fifteenth time, I was watching the match at home. I really wanted him to win, because it made me feel like a kid again. It brought a little bit of respectability back to WCW at a down time for our company. I remember the time I wrestled him in Minneapolis, on April 25, 1999. I had speared him and had him up in the Jackhammer when he said to me, "Billy, remember two things: I'm fifty years old and I love you. So be careful." I had to do everything in my power to keep from cracking up.

The Wrestling So-Called Business

When I signed my deal in April of 1998, Eric Bischoff told me that if things went well we could renegotiate my contract. By March of 1999, things were going very well, and I felt that I should be paid accordingly, and so did my agents, Barry Bloom and Michael Braverman. I hired a high-profile sports attorney, Henry Holmes, and we were in the middle of renegotiations when a product tie-in commercial fiasco came up. As I sit here and write from the house that WCW built, it's obvious that I've benefited from my experience.

I was recovering from knee surgery and sitting with my brother Steve at a Stanley Cup game in Dallas when my pager went off. WCW was insisting that I appear the next day in a product tie-in commercial, and telling me I was obligated to do so under my contract. Barry and Henry saw it differently. Although my contract called for me to do promotions for WCW, I was not required to do third-party product endorsements. But the WCW told me I'd be in breach of my contract if I didn't appear. They added that if I did appear, and I returned to the ring right away, they would come to the table and finish the deal.

Barry and Henry told me I should show up for the commercial, but that whatever I did, I shouldn't sign anything. Signing a release would hinder our bargaining position. I left early the next morning, went back to Atlanta, and did the commercial. Sure enough, there was a release for me to sign, and I said no way. Since I wouldn't sign the paper, the WCW people wouldn't come to the table on Tuesday to renegotiate as promised. So on went months and months of the renegotiations, complete with threats from both sides. It was an arduous process. Finally, they offered me a certain amount of money for the commercial if I agreed to come back. I started thinking maybe I should throw these guys a bone, maybe I ought to make it right. I figured I'd take what they were offering me, bury the hatchet, and go back to work. I told them I'd think about it seriously, and I called Barry and Henry to get their opinions. They laughed at me,

Page and Kanyon—pros at making someone look like a million bucks.

and thinking about it now, I'm laughing for the same reason. The WCW offer was ridiculously low. They had already aired the commercial without my consent, and Henry felt confident that we could initiate legal proceedings that would render my contract null and void. In the end, they gave me much more than the amount that Bischoff had offered me originally for the commercial. By the way, I also got a renegotiated contract. WCW finally stepped up.

Unfortunately, the real victim in the deal was Meng. He's a great guy and a terrific family man. He's got a number of kids and supposedly, because of his contract, he received very little to do the commercial. I thought that was ridiculous, and to me this exemplified how unfair the business of pro wrestling can be. They should have paid Meng more for his time, and I ended up giving him part of what I received. I didn't do this because I felt sorry for him, but because he deserved it. In fact, Meng stole the commercial. *He* was the star.

Sid Vicious

When I came back from my knee injury, my next really big feud was with Sid Vicious. Sid is believable in the ring, except that he is a little immobile because of his injuries. With his look and his intensity, that's money, as they say in the business. He's established as a character, and he's a good guy. Sid is a simple man from Arkansas. He takes a lot of pride in what he does, which I respect, and I'm very happy that he found something that got him away from Arkansas.

I was wrestling Sid for the U.S. belt in Las Vegas at *Halloween Havoc* on October 24, 1999. The match barely got started when it had to be stopped because of Sid's excessive blood loss. I'm not too much in favor of giving blood for a match. Though I felt bad for Sid the whole time, and I would have rathered it was me bleeding, believe me, it was kind of a cool feeling, that blood bath. I know it's weird to say. I've never gigged myself in the ring—I usually give my blood without having to try. To me, it is exhilarating to bleed. As gross as it may sound, I revel in the fact that blood, whether it's mine or someone else's, is flowing. I just get off on it.

Referee Mickey Jay:

During the Sid Vicious match at Halloween Havoc in Vegas, well, I was the one that cut Sid, because he hadn't done it before. And I wasn't too thrilled about doing it because I thought, hell, I'd gladly do it to myself, but not to somebody else. During the match, they kept telling me in the earpiece in the back, "We need more." They wanted me to cut him again. There wasn't any way that I was going to do that, so I went over to Bill. He had him in a headlock or something and I told him to take his fist and punch him in the head and hard. Like this. And I hit my own hand. Bill kind of looked at me, and he did it.

The pay-per-view ended with Sting issuing an open challenge, which I accepted. I went out and beat him for my second World Title, even though it was taken away the next night on a technicality. That was the first WCW pay-per-view with Vince Russo in charge. He adds a dimension to our show that many people think it needs. He brings the World Wrestling Federation's style of entertainment down to WCW, which I suppose the WCW was lacking. In the beginning, I definitely think he went a bit overboard. There's a time and place for

A night to remember.

everything, and I don't like all the T and A on our show, because it's not suited for the kids. Russo is extremely creative, and very passionate about the business. He is a huge asset as long as his talents are exploited properly and they don't overwhelm the show. He is a very important piece of the puzzle, but he is not the only piece. A number of different styles and philosophies need to be bound together to come up with a product that satisfies and entertains everyone out there.

Bret Hart

Bret Hart has wrestling in his blood, and he's been in the business a long time. I feel terrible for the guy because of all the problems he's had. He got screwed over by the World Wrestling Federation, he's had injury problems, and what happened to his brother is a real shame.

Back in April 1999, in Toronto, at the first *Nitro* ever held in Canada, a storyline issue began between Bret Hart and me. Bret came out and cut a vicious promo against WCW, saying how much it sucked and how he wanted to leave. He called me out and I speared him. But Bret got up and I stayed down. It turned out that he was wearing a metal plate to defend himself against the move. It was brutal. Bret was supposed to be the heel and I was supposed to be the baby face, but since we were in serious Bret Hart country, it didn't quite work out that way. Bret's a national hero in Canada, after all. Unfortunately, the storyline between Bret and me never went anywhere. And then in the fall, things got kind of confusing. We were the Tag Team Champions for about fifteen minutes, then we had a couple of matches against each other. On the *Nitro* after I won both belts, I was stripped of the World Title because my match against Sting wasn't a "sanctioned" match. A World Title tournament began, and I faced Bret in the first round, with my U.S. Title on the line. He wound up getting a bogus win with help from Nash and Hall. Help that he supposedly didn't want. He went on to win the tournament and the title at the next pay-per-view, *Mayhem*, which was also held in Toronto. I wrestled Sid in an I Quit match, and I won, but the fans in Toronto were still booing me because of the heat between Bret and me. They probably booed me because they felt so sorry for Bret since I had recently beat him from ring post to ring post. They could do nothing but boo.

Bret and I were scheduled to wrestle once again at *Starrcade* on December 19 in Washington, D.C. We were having a pretty good match until Roddy Piper came out and rang the bell prematurely when Bret had me in his finishing move, the Sharpshooter, and declared Bret the winner. I thought the whole thing was a lame way

to finish off what's supposed to be the biggest pay-per-view of the year, and the fans were pissed off by it, too.

The other notable thing from that match was that Bret got a concussion when I kicked him in the head. I just hope that he gets better. It was completely by accident and I'm very sorry that it happened. Everyone who's ever been in the ring with me knows I'd rather hurt myself than someone else. I've heard rumors that Bret thinks I threw

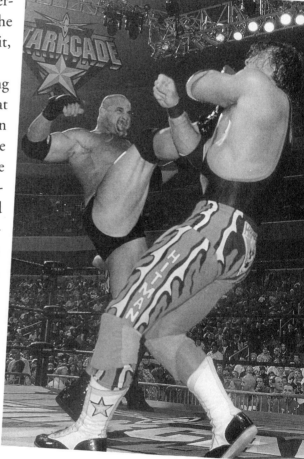

Giving the boot to Bret Hart.

the kick with malice. That's bullshit, and Bret knows that's bullshit. So I've still never had a legitimate match with Bret. He's either been cast as a cheater or whatever. And I'd really enjoy a match against him with a decent ending and no interference. I'd love to go toe-to-toe with Bret, because I could learn a lot from him.

The Injury

Unfortunately, sometimes I go too far, like when I put my arm through a limousine window and severed my tendons. I came within two centimeters of screwing myself up permanently, but part of me still thinks it was a great way to go out. I know it's dumb thinking like that, and I don't know if it's the showman in me or the devil in me or the stupid guy in me or what.

First of all, the window should have been made with fake glass. The script called for me to bust the windows with a sledgehammer, but that's silly. My girlfriend could break a window with a sledgehammer. Where's the theatrics in that? Goldberg doesn't do things like everybody else. Goldberg does things with his frickin' fists . . . which is the way I busted those windows. I had a real-life confrontation with Scott Hall earlier in the night, and I envisioned his face being those limousine windows as I sliced right through them. In reality, looking back on it, I think I knew that I was going to get hurt. I didn't care. I wanted to kill something, and being the professional that I am, I didn't want to drop Scott Hall like a sack of potatoes backstage, but maybe that's what I should have done. Well, there's always next time. I bled for three and a half hours before they could stop it. It was pretty nasty. I appreciated all of those guys being there—Rick Steiner, Russo, Ed Ferrara, and my girlfriend, Lisa. Steiner had to pull my damn pants off in the hospital. He stayed with me the whole time, and flew with me the next day, and so did Lisa. I didn't ask Steiner to do that, but he did it, and I'll be forever grateful. I can't explain to you how much I love that guy.

I ended up with 196 stitches, and six months away from
wrestling. Just three years before, I was out of work, had no idea
where my life was headed, and most people didn't know me from
Adam. Now I finally had time to sit back and reflect on how drastically everything had changed. There was no turning back.

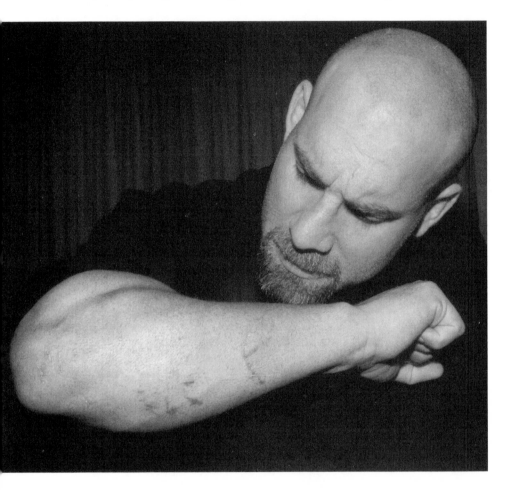

chapter eight

THINGS CHANGE

I became a celebrity overnight. I don't know how, and I still don't understand why. The first time I was publicly recognized happened as I was getting off a plane—a gentleman from across the hall called my name. He was a tall, black gentleman, and he looked familiar, but I couldn't tell who he was until he got up close. I looked at him and realized that he was George Wallace, the comedian. He told me that he was a big fan of mine, and I was floored, because to be perfectly honest with you, I think he is one of the funniest guys on the planet. That's when I was like, "Man, I must be doing something right because George Wallace knows who I am."

George Wallace:

I saw him on TV. I go, boy, this guy's really talented and can dish out some entertainment. Then I met him walking through the Atlanta airport one day, in front of Gate A19.

People began recognizing me everywhere. It's no big deal to me, and it doesn't make me better than anyone else. Although it is strange, it's not difficult to put in perspective. We're on TV five hours a week in addition to our monthly pay-per-views, so we're shoved down people's throats. Athletes have always been revered, and as sports entertainers, wrestlers are revered as well. The fact that a person can be so successful and so well known through professional wrestling is hilarious to me. But it's really not any stranger than anything else. The whole world is pretty goofy.

My popularity began to snowball when I started winning more matches, which led to more mainstream publicity. I was getting a lot of attention from the media, and my picture began showing up in various publications. Although it was nice to be mentioned in *The New Yorker,* I was especially pleased to find myself on the cover of *Cracked* magazine . . . twice.

The *New Yorker* article broached a subject that was becoming common knowledge. People were picking up on the fact that with a name like Goldberg, I might be Jewish. Although there were other Jewish professional wrestlers (Scott Levy, A.K.A. Raven; Dean Simon, A.K.A. Dean Malenko; Barry Horowitz, A.K.A. Barry Horowitz), I was being touted as the next Sandy Koufax. This was quite an honor, albeit one that I hardly deserved. Thanks to the tremendous media coverage, my popularity was skyrocketing. It's funny, because people have actually come up to me and asked if Goldberg is my real name. How do you answer that question with a straight face?

At the beginning I thought that being Jewish would be a detriment, and I didn't want to make it an issue, and I never would have let WCW make it an issue. Fortunately, they didn't bring it up. I wasn't trying to hide my religion, and I knew that it was going to come out in the open eventually. When someone did make an issue out of my religion, it was because other Jews liked the fact that I was a wrestler. I was surprised. I thought they'd shun me for it.

I imagined that people wouldn't cheer for me. That they'd see nothing but a big Jewish guy out there, with long, curly sideburns; wearing a big yarmulke; carrying a huge Torah; spinning in the ring like a dreidel. I wasn't very objective about it, and maybe I was narrow-minded. The fans aren't concerned about religion, they're interested in the entertainment value of one's character. After the chant began, it was strange going into auditoriums throughout the Deep South and hearing people chant, *"Goldberg . . . Goldberg,"* and not one of them was wearing a white hood and carrying a noose.

I'm proud to say that I have never encountered anti-Semitism in the wrestling arena, nor have I noticed prejudice toward other minority wrestlers. How do I feel about being Jewish? About the same way I feel about being from Oklahoma. You don't choose your heritage. I feel a strong sense of my history, but I feel no better or worse than anyone else, as long as they are a good person.

I have received various honors and awards from Jewish organizations. I've been asked to give out awards at the Maccabee games in Israel, and to speak at the Young Jewish Men's conference. The Jewish National Fund wants me to dedicate a water project in Israel, and I was offered a ride over there on the Estee Lauder family plane.

As we're writing this, I'm playing with the necklace that Hallie Eisenberg gave me at the American Music Awards. She's the cute little girl on the Pepsi commercials. It's great to be in a position to be a role model for little kids. It's also great to be in a position to be a role model to a group of kids who are in a minority. Especially since I didn't have any Jewish idols (I guess I wasn't supposed to worship idols) growing up, except my brothers, Mike and Steve. I don't exactly fit the Jewish stereotype. One thing's for sure, when I do decide to give up wrestling, I could have a long and profitable career on the Bar Mitzvah circuit.

I knew that I had arrived when Adam Sandler told me that I have

David Arquette and Adam Sandler—two great guys, then there's me.

attained more for the Jewish religion as a wrestler than his Hanukkah song. I don't know if I believe him, but I do think it's pretty damn funny.

Things really started to change when I hit mainstream TV. I was on *The Tonight Show with Jay Leno, Live with Regis and Kathie Lee, Politically Incorrect,* and *Dennis Miller Live.* I even had a guest appearance on *The Love Boat.* And then I broke into the movies, costarring with Jean-Claude Van Damme in the blockbuster *Universal Soldier . . . the Return.*

Jean-Claude Van Damme, Lisa, and me.

Goldberg's Famous Friends

When I was just a little kid, I used to watch Jose Cruz play baseball for the minor league Tulsa Drillers. He played outfield and he batted left-handed with a big stutter step. Watching him play was one of my great childhood memories. A couple of years ago, when I took batting practice with Montreal, Jose Cruz was pitching. I went long. I've had the chance to take batting practice with a number of major league teams and I've gone yard in a lot of places.

I got a phone call one afternoon inviting me to go out and meet Mark McGwire through some friends of mine, the Rubensteins. They lived in Fort Lauderdale and they were friends with Ron Gant, who was McGwire's teammate on the Cardinals. I partied with Gant a couple of times when I was with the Falcons and he was with the Braves. He relayed the message to me that McGwire's kid was a Goldberg fan. We were in Miami for a *Nitro* and the Marlins were playing the Cardinals. I was running around the locker room looking for someone to give me approval to leave the arena and go to the game. This was during the time when I wouldn't leave the grounds until I got someone's O.K. So I grabbed Jimmy Hart and explained the situation and he said, "What, are you kidding me? Let's grab a camera guy and a driver and get the hell over there." No matter what happened, we'd make it back in time for the show, so we decided to take the chance. We ended out on the field and there was McGwire. I was wearing my Goldberg shirt and he came over and we started talking. It was a few days before he broke the record and

NASCAR legend Darrell Waltrip.

it was an opportunity that never in a million years would I have expected. He rubbed his bat on my chest for good luck and lo and behold a few days later, he broke the record. This was a moment that I'll never forget. It was a hell of an honor. And so was having him hit after me during batting practice at another game. Another time, I was down in the pit area during the Pepsi 400 at Daytona, next to Wally Dallenbach, who drives for WCW. Someone came over from Darrell Waltrip's crew and said that Darrell would like to talk to me. He was going to retire after the season and this was his last appearance at Daytona, so there were a lot of people around him. We had met briefly before and he just wanted to tell me that he had heard from everybody down in the pit area that I was a nice guy and he thought that I was one of the best representatives for my business that he had ever seen. It was incredible to get a compliment like that from someone who's such a great representative for his own business. He's a legend, man. He's one of the best ever.

Steve, Brett Hull, and me after a 1999 Stanley Cup Game.

I'm frequently cast in these situations, and they still seem quite strange to me. I really enjoy watching hockey, and because I'm Goldberg the wrestler, I was able to stand next to Wayne Gretzky the night before his induction into the Hockey Hall of Fame. I've been a big fan of Brett Hull's for years. I'd only been to one hockey game in the past, and he gave me the opportunity to take my brother Steve to a Stanley Cup game. I first met Brett when he and a few of his teammates came to *Nitro* in Dallas. The next night there was a hockey game. I attended the game and was honored to go out to dinner with a number of the guys afterward. I met his wife and kids, and some time later I was doing a Coors promotion alongside his father, hockey legend Bobby Hull. He's in the Hockey Hall of Fame, and he might have been the greatest hockey player that ever lived. This is a guy that never in a trillion years would I have had a chance to meet, let alone hang out with. Now all of the barriers are broken down, and these guys treat me like a human being, which is all you can ask for.

I used to watch the original "Awesome" Bill Elliot from behind a fence, and now I'm driving down the street with him in the town where we both live in his personal six-hundred-horsepower Cobra. I went from being Bill Goldberg from Tulsa to being the next "Awesome" Bill from Dawsonville, though I could never hold a candle to the great Mr. Elliot. Just knowing what great people he and his family are is a great honor. Thanks, Bill.

I've always wanted to be on *Dennis Miller Live,* and when I found out that he was a fan, I introduced myself to him and his kids at a show in L.A. I told him that I'd love to be on his show—a few months later, there I was.

Dennis Miller:

Goldberg always seemed like a good guy to me. We went to the Great Western Forum and we met him backstage, and it was like the best thing that could happen for my kids, because they could see that these guys were real human beings. Not only were they real human beings, but I've never, never been with any celebrity or athlete with my children that was nicer than these guys. They are so thoughtful with the young kids. I was really touched by it.

Years ago, the closest I would have come to boxing champ Vinny Pazienza might have been getting into a fight with him in a bar in Las Vegas. Now that I'm Goldberg, I've escorted him into the ring.

I sat with Evander Holyfield's kids during one of his fights. I played in a charity golf tournament with Michael Jordan. Who would have thought that I'd be playing in a golf tournament with Jordan, and have people comparing the size of my gallery to his? It turned out that there were more people following me than him. Of course, this might be because he restricts the number of autographs he signs. Who knows. Speaking of Jordan, there is a marketing company in New York that conducts surveys to determine the popularity and marketability of celebrities and athletes. The result is called the Q rating. Michael Jordan had the highest Q rating in the country for ten years. At one point in 1998, he dropped to number two behind . . . yes, as strange as it may seem, it was Goldberg the wrestler.

Charles Barkley, Karl Malone, and Shaquille O'Neal are fans. When I was one of the presenters at the American Music Awards, I ran into Shaq after the event. He was walking down the street, and I had the limo driver pull over so I could ask Shaq for his autograph. When he looked in and saw me he said, "Goldberg! Let me get an autograph, man!"

There are people in other sports that I used to look up to, who now are watching me because their kids are fans of mine. Talk about a weird feeling. I get a hoot out of thinking about that. Jerry Rice introduced his kids to me, and he was smiling because they were so

My friend Ricky Medlocke of Lynyrd Skynyrd.

happy to meet me. Brett Hull, Chuck Norris, Mark McGwire, Howie Long, Karl Malone, and Dennis Miller all have kids who are fans.

Teammate Tim Green:

I have young kids. My boys are ten and five. When I was a kid, I used to run around with my friends and say, "I'm Superman. I'm Batman!" Those were like the ultimate superheroes! Well, my kids run around saying, "I'm GOLDBERG!"

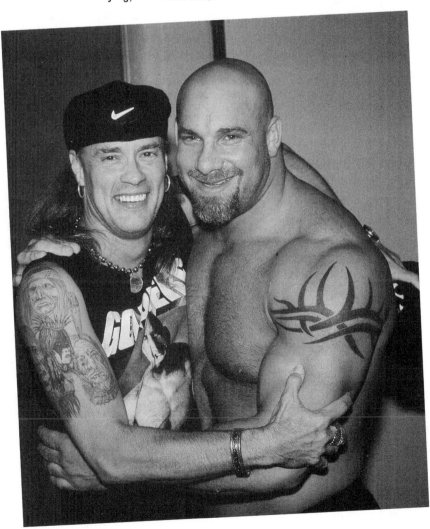

Having great football players think that what I do is cool is really special for me. These are guys who I idolize because they're succeeding at something that I tried to do and came up short. John Randall, Gilbert Brown, and Warren Sapp are fans. And I'm a big fan of theirs, too.

John Randall:

If I were a wrestler, I'd be Goldberg. I'd have a goatee and swing my arms up like he does. He played in the NFL, and when I first saw him it was like, Yeah! He's got real game. He's living my dream in wrestling. Can I get a signed copy of the book?

It was awesome being able to take batting practice with Jeff Bagwell and to have the chance to throw out the first pitch at an Astros game. It was also pretty great having him go around and get autographs for me from his teammates. I don't know what these

With Craig Biggio, Ken Caminiti, and Jeff Bagwell.

guys see in me, but I'm glad they see something, because hanging out with them is a dream come true. Some teams have quite a few guys who are fans, like the Cincinnati Reds. It's cool to hang out with guys like Danny Graves and Ken Griffey, Jr. Jason Giambi of the A's is also a fan and a friend. John Rocker even wore my shirt during the World Series. I guess he doesn't know I'm Jewish.

One time when I was in Sturgis, South Dakota, for the *Road Wild* pay-per-view, I rode my Harley to my first motorcycle rally. We drove to a field to hear Lynyrd Skynyrd in concert. We couldn't get into the back area, because even though we'd left our names, they weren't on the list. Some security guy was giving us a hard time, and band member Ricky Medlock ran out of the van, screaming and yelling to let us in. He's a very close friend and a truly great guy. He started hugging me, and we talked for a while, then I proceeded to the pit to watch the concert. For an encore, Ricky came out wearing a Goldberg shirt during "Free Bird," and I hear he does that all the time. What an honor. When I was a special guest of the Miami Heat, I looked up and saw Jimmy Buffett was wearing a Goldberg hat.

Jimmy Buffett:

My son Cameron is a huge Goldberg fan. We've got Goldberg underwear, shirts, dolls—Goldberg everything!

Unfortunately, I don't have the time that I once had for my buddies. And they're probably happy about that, because when I didn't have a job, they probably saw a lot more of me than they wanted to. On the other hand, it's great that I can have a house in California and can take my friends out there and share things with them. I've wanted to do that since I was a kid. We hang out at my place near the beach, and it's like having our own playground. But the negative part is that not only do I have less time to do those things, sometimes those friends are caught in the middle of people trying to get in touch with me for various reasons. That happens with my family members, too.

Things have also changed with my family. Before I started wrestling, I was only acquainted with my semi-immediate family, but when I became Goldberg, I suddenly had cousins that I never knew existed. And *distant* relatives surfaced throughout the country. I had people coming out of the woodwork who had never contacted me until I became somebody from wrestling. I have to change my phone numbers every three months. I don't give a flying flip who I give my double-secret probation number to, because every three months it's going to change. It's a pain in the butt. But when the phone stops ringing, then something's wrong.

The Kids

By far, the most important part of my success is that it gives me the opportunity to make a difference with kids. I didn't have too much of a chance to do this when I was playing football. Even though I played in the NFL, because football is a team sport, only a certain number of players are recognized publicly—mostly superstars. Wrestling is a completely different story, because you are marketed on your individuality. In most professional athletics, this is not the case. Kids get lost in wrestlers because they look at us like comic book superheroes. We're like Superman. We're able to do these spectacular things in and out of the ring, and be this invincible force. It makes perfect sense that kids look up to us.

Wrestling gave me the opportunity to be a role model; football didn't give me that. I do what I do now because I get to put smiles on kids' faces. And that's worth everything to me. It's worth more than money, and I can say that with conviction. Money's great, don't get me wrong, but watching a kid who doesn't have much time to live go from a shy introvert in excruciating pain to an extroverted playful kid again—seemingly painless, seemingly careless—that's magic. That turns me into a magician. And that right there is the best thing in the world. Living in this house is great, being able to have my own plane is great, being able to have my picture on this or that is great. But being able to help people is something I've never been able to do before. I can now help members of my family, and my friends, and that's great and all—but the feeling I get from making kids happy, that's priceless.

With my brave friend, Adrian Martinez.

Before, I could maybe affect a kid whose parents went to the University of Georgia, who maybe watched me play football. After I became Goldberg the wrestler, not only could I put smiles on kids' faces, I was a recipient of requests from the Make-A-Wish Foundation. That's pretty heavy. To be the recipient of a Make-A-Wish request is something else that wouldn't have happened before. And this is sometimes a weekly occurrence for me now. Although it's something that I'm extremely proud of, I hardly feel deserving of this honor (responsibility?). Who am I? But as long as I'm able to make some kid happy, I'll continue to do it. You put smiles on these kids' faces and you grant their wishes. But the unfortunate part is that you get so close to them that god forbid something happens, you feel as if you've lost a member of your family. So there's a great deal of pain along with the joy. I still have yet to figure out how to deal with that pain. I have talked to former tennis star Andrea Jaeger, who has been a very big help, as have Bill and Ernie Elliot and Kenny Bernstein.

Bill Elliot, being the recipient of the most popular driver award many times, really knows how to deal with people. Andrea is the same way. Look what she's done with her Silver Lining Foundation in Aspen. They help kids with cancer and other serious illnesses enjoy their lives more. My brother Mike got me involved with them three years ago. Andrea had a career-ending shoulder injury, and she decided to dedicate her life to this cause. She needs to be commended. I'm also actively involved with the Special Olympics, Karl Malone's Foundation for Kids, the American Diabetes Association, the Juvenile Diabetes Foundation, Angela's House, National D.A.R.E., and Kmart Kids Race Against Drugs.

One thing that I've learned by being around these kids is how to control my emotions. You have to realize that kids are affected by your actions, so if you react to them with surprise or fear or sorrow or if you're overly sympathetic, they pick up on that. And then they think that you're feeling sorry for them. I take on an entirely different character when I go in there. Whether it's the way that I talk or react or look, I try to control my emotions and be a happy, very pleasing individual. I'll do anything I can for these kids. I'm the most subservient of any time in my life during the time I spend with these kids.

Some of Goldberg's Friends

I'd like to introduce you to my friend Adrian Martinez. I was on the road preparing to go to a match, and I was watching HBO. This kid was on TV, and he was wearing a Goldberg shirt and he was lying on a Goldberg bedspread. I became interested, so I listened to his

My darling
Brianna.

story, and it was about kids who were abused by authority figures. Adrian was abused by his baseball coach, and he spoke out against him and stood up and held his ground. He set an example for all of these other kids, whether they were on that baseball team or somewhere else. He's such a brave kid, I just had to get ahold of him. I contacted him, and now we're friends. We talk a couple of times a month. I even flew to Vegas to surprise him at his birthday party.

Brianna is a six-year-old little girl who was a Make-A-Wish recipient. She wore Goldberg: shorts, wristband, shirt, and socks. They brought her in in a wheelchair, and she was a real introvert. You have to feel these kids out and do whatever you can to try to make them break out of their shell. One thing led to another, and she was all over me and I was all over her. It was great. We got tickets for Brianna and her family, and they ended up watching the show with us on a monitor in the back. Sid Vicious came back there with us, and she loved Sid, too. She's awesome! I carry pictures of these kids in my briefcase to put a smile on my face. I met with her at a *Nitro* in St. Louis to fly her and her family to my comeback match in Atlanta.

Unfortunately, I've lost a few kids. I met Chad Dunn through Karl Malone and his Karl Malone's Foundation for Kids. Chad had cancer, and he lost his leg to the disease. He went through bone marrow transplants, and his parents were by his side the whole time. He fought his whole life. He never felt sorry for himself. He didn't bitch, moan, or complain. I knew him for three years, and he was one of my best friends. I hope I was able to ease his pain. In reality he did more for me than I ever did for him. He grounded me. He made my fast-paced life slow down a bit so I could keep things in perspective. I miss you very much, Chad, you'll always be the man.

How do I deal with the pain and sadness? A couple of times I've left the room with these kids and broken down. And then I'll go off and punch something, out of frustration. Other times, I've dealt with it through wrestling. When I'm in the ring, as controlled and choreographed as what we do is, and as much as I'm trying to take care of the guy I'm wrestling, I'm also trying to kill him. I'm looking through the eyes of these kids. So there are ways that I can use wrestling as an outlet for my aggression, without really hurting people.

I take my success for what it's worth. And I do understand that I have an obligation to the public when I walk out of my house. Since they look at me as Goldberg the wrestler, I'm going to be smart enough and respectful enough to provide them with a role model that people can look up to. Anything short of that would be letting my fans down, and not fulfilling my obligation. I always take time for the public, but there's a time and a place for everything. I don't like being bothered by an adult when I'm eating my dinner or working out or doing something like that. That's just common courtesy. But I honestly can't think of many situations where I wouldn't stop to give a kid an autograph. I feel bad when I hear that some people assume that celebrities give autographs solely for monetary gain. I do it for the kids, not for the publicity. Publicity's nice, and being cheered is nice, and winning a lot of wrestling matches is fine and dandy. But it doesn't make me a better person. What I hope makes me a better person is trying to do something for other people.

Chad Dunn and his good friend.

I do charity work for various other organizations, as well. I've always been a huge animal lover. Now I'm in a position to make a difference by adopting god knows how many animals. I mean, I'm not at home right now, so there's probably one more. I'm a spokesperson for the Humane Society of the United States, and I've spoken on Capitol Hill for animal rights. I do public service announcements for the Humane Society because throughout my life animals have always been there for me. Animals have been my best friends during various times of my life, and I love them for it.

Goldberg's Public Service Announcement

People need to understand their responsibility when they have a pet.

Please neuter your pet, because there are millions of unwanted pets killed each year because of overpopulation.

The problem is that there are so many charities out there that need attention, but you only have time to do so much. I try to choose causes that have affected me personally. I'd like to start helping the elderly, because my grandparents weren't alive long enough for me to really know them. Maybe that will give me a chance to fill that void.

I was reminded of my grandparents in a haunting way by an encounter with an elderly fan at the United States Holocaust Memorial Museum in Washington, D.C. I had just finished an emotional tour of the museum, and as we were walking toward the exit, I stopped to enroll as a donor. The woman in charge of memberships asked me my name, and when I told her it was Goldberg, she recognized me and was instantly overcome with joy. She was hugging me and telling me that her grandchildren were big fans, and that it was an honor for her to meet such an important Jew. I noticed the numbers tattooed on her wrist, and a feeling of great sorrow overwhelmed me as I realized that this person had lived and survived the horror that I had just observed. Seeing exhibits and pictures was one thing, but to actually meet and touch someone who was there made it real. How could such a brave person think that I was so special? I looked at her and told her that I was honored to be in her presence, and that she was the one who was important.

Full Circle

Because of the large difference in our ages, my brother Mike was always kind of like another father to me. When I first told him about my decision to become a professional wrestler, his response was less than enthusiastic. Just a couple of years later, he was pretending to be me.

Mike as me—whoever would have thought?

Mike Goldberg:

My kids' school put on their annual play and it covered pop culture through the year 2000. They asked me if I could get Bill to play himself, and I said, "I don't think so." So they said, "Would you play him?" I said sure, so when I told my kids I was going to play Uncle Billy, they said, "Dad, you have to shave your head!"

I came out of the audience wearing a leather jacket and a ball cap. All of a sudden, Bill's introduction music started playing, and the spotlight focused on me. One of the teachers started taunting me, and two of my sons joined me as bodyguards. They were wearing police uniforms, and they escorted me to the stage. The teacher and I started wrestling, and we danced around a little. We had practiced the moves a couple of times, and he flipped me on my back. He jumped on top of me, and I kicked him off and turned him over and pinned him. There was a real cute teacher who acted as the ring girl, so I picked her up and carried her off-stage. Then the kids started the Goldberg chant, and I came back out and pointed to the audience and said, "Don't try this at home!"

The funny part about this is that all the little kids, the first-graders, thought that I was really Goldberg. They asked me for my autograph—or really, Bill's autograph. Bill used to be my brother, but I guess now I'm his.

chapter nine

ONE SUPER SUNDAY

by Steve Goldberg

Bill didn't want to write this chapter himself because he was kind of embarrassed by all that went on. But I was there, and it went something like this.

In 1984, Jed, Mike, and I took Bill to Super Bowl XVIII in Tampa. We flew up from Miami, and as we were approaching the stadium, my dad asked Mike where the tickets were, and Mike replied, "What tickets? We don't have tickets." Tickets had never been a problem for Mike in the past, since he'd always been able to scalp them before the big game. But that year in Tampa was a different story. Tampa Stadium was considerably smaller than other NFL venues, and tickets were not to be found. We returned to the airport, caught a flight back to Miami, and we arrived at Mike's house in time to watch the second half.

A couple of years ago, Bill couldn't get an NFL team to return his phone call. In 1999 the league invited him to Super Bowl XXXIII as their guest! Many times, Bill had tagged along to major events with Jed, Mike, and me. He was thrilled to finally be able to return the favor and bring us along on the adventure with him!

It all began on Friday in San Diego. Bill was scheduled to wrestle there that night. The next day, he had to go to L.A. for a commercial shoot and another match. He was then scheduled to appear on *Nitro* in Minneapolis on Monday. The Super Bowl was on Sunday. In exchange for appearing at the game and signing autographs at the NFL Experience, he was given four tickets, one for each of the Goldberg boys. We were ready for a weekend of wrestling, football, and a whole lot of fun.

It was a perfect setup. I own restaurants in San Diego and Minneapolis; Mike had business meetings in L.A., and our father, Jed, lives in Miami, the site of Super Bowl XXXIII. Logistics? *No problemo.* Mike owns and flies a Cessna Citation X, the fastest business jet in the world.

Squaring off with Nash in San Diego.

On Friday, we met for lunch at my restaurant in Solana Beach, the Pacific Coast Grill, to plan the trip. The bar on the plane was fully stocked and we had plenty of food, so we were ready to go. All Bill had to do was survive the matches and we'd be off to Miami.

The Friday night house show in San Diego featured Goldberg and Kevin Nash in the main event. It was a short match—Bill quickly dispatched Kevin with a spear and the Jackhammer. He showered and changed, signed autographs, and posed for pictures. Then we headed back to the restaurant for a late-night dinner. We ate and drank and relaxed, and after a while, we were off to get a few hours of sleep before heading to L.A.

Bill had to be on the set for the commercial shoot in L.A. by ten A.M., and we didn't get to bed until two. Mike had left his plane in L.A., but fortunately an old friend of his, Jep Thornton, had come with him to San Diego. Jep offered to fly us to Burbank in his jet. The twenty-minute flight beat the hell out of a two-and-a-half-hour drive. We were met at the airport by the Boyz II Men stretch limo. Boyz II Men were out of town, but the Goldberg Boys were just arriving.

We arrived at the Hollywood Center Studio, and Bill was whisked off to makeup and then to the set for shooting. His scene consisted of opening his mouth and acting as if he was catching a piece of candy that sent his head recoiling back. Then he was supposed to growl, then smile and express satisfaction. This was done on a soundstage in front of a green background that enabled a computer to insert the candy and generate the background at a later date. After about an hour of grunting and smiling, the shoot was a wrap, and Bill had just scored some easy dough.

As we were walking off the set, Sarah Michelle Gellar, A.K.A. Buffy the Vampire Slayer, came up and introduced herself to Bill. "It's great to meet you and have you here on the set," she said. Having been up most of the night, we felt fortunate that she didn't put a stake through our hearts! We went directly from Buffy to the buffet, where we ate enough to hold us over until lunch. Only in Hollywood do you find vitamins, supplements, and holistic remedies on the buffet table.

Bill was in need of a workout, and when he's in L.A., that means Gold's Gym in Venice Beach. He needed more fuel, so we piled into the Boyz II Men mobile in search of sushi.

Bill ordered four orders of tuna sashimi, four orders of eel, miso soup, and the tempura vegetable and chicken combination. Then he went across the street to the Beverly Center to buy a pair of dress shoes. Because of his hectic travel schedule and his size, Bill generally wears the most comfortable clothes available, but on Tuesday he was scheduled to speak to the United States Congress as spokesman for the Humane Society. Somewhere along the way, he had to find a dress shirt with a twenty-two-inch collar, to complete his wardrobe.

I was probably the smallest guy at Gold's Gym in Venice Beach.

Entering Gold's Gym is like stepping into the bar scene in *Star Wars*. There were both men and women there, all comically pumped up out of proportion. The word had spread that Bill would be working out there, so a number of people had assembled outside, waiting for autographs and pictures. He told them that he would be happy to accommodate them after his workout. Bill doesn't like to be interrupted during his workout routine. The gym is his office, and he takes his work very seriously.

The crowd outside had grown considerably, and we stayed long enough for Bill to sign every autograph and pose for every picture request. We finally boarded the limo, and we were off in search of more food. We went to a local health-food bar and grill, where Bill ordered a protein shake and a double chicken breast and rice. He doesn't like to eat too much before his matches.

We arrived at the Forum to hundreds of fans hoping to get a glimpse of the wrestlers. Bill was interviewed by E! TV and a local news station. Afterward, he was taken upstairs to meet a couple of fans, who turned out to be Dennis Miller and Rita Rudner. Their kids were big fans, too, and Bill signed autographs for them all. Backstage was full of a cross section of Hollywood types. There were actors, producers, and agents, all of whom wanted to be part of the action. Bill's match was with Nash again—and it was spear, Jackhammer, and off to the Super Bowl!

As we left the arena, the road was lined with people waiting for the wrestlers to emerge. In general, wrestling crowds just want to see and meet their heroes. But this group was rude and obnoxious, shouting obscenities and making lewd gestures. It was a strange scene, and we were anxious to get out of there.

The Game

We arrived at LAX and loaded up the Citation X. It was approaching midnight, and we were all looking forward to a little rest before the big game. All of us except Mike, who was anxious to get behind the wheel of his rocket ship. The Citation X will fly at .92 mach (over six hundred miles per hour) and cruise at over fifty thousand feet.

We had picked up another couple of passengers along the way—Scott "Big Poppa Pump" Steiner, the man with the biggest biceps in all of wrestling, and his girlfriend. Scott didn't have a ticket to the game, or a hotel room, but he wanted to go along for the ride and the festivities in Miami. Soon we were climbing into the black sky, and the Pacific faded away behind us. Three hours and fifty-two minutes later, we awoke to the sun rising over the Atlantic and Miami, just a short descent away.

We checked into our hotel for a couple more hours of sleep, and then we were off again. We had sent our limo to stock up on beer and pick up our father in Coconut Grove. It was wonderful for us to be together again, and we started our celebration at our favorite Miami restaurant, Joe's Stone Crab. We reminisced about our previous adventures in Miami, thanks to Mike, who lived there in the eighties. Our older brother has provided a lot of fun for our family with all of his generosity and toys. Miami had been a jumping-off point for many trips to the Caribbean, and Mike always had a cool sailboat to take us there. By the end of the meal, Scott and Bill had attracted a crowd at the table, including a few seasoned waiters who were huge fans.

Scott had a friend in town, and we proceeded to meet up with him on his 119-foot motor sailer. The crowd was very Southern and a bit conservative, but very hospitable. I was talking to a guy about wrestling, and he commented that it was a big draw for his family's company. "Why, we even have a commercial during the Super Bowl," he commented. As we were leaving, I asked who the guy was, and Scott informed me that it was Ted Turner's son. It was pretty funny that the son of the founder of Turner Television (which, through their parent company Time Warner, owns WCW wrestling) wasn't aware that it was the World Wrestling Federation, not the WCW, that was airing the commercial.

**Brother Steve and I trying
to talk each other out of writing the book.**

We headed for the stadium, and we sorely missed the Boyz II Men limo. Our current car was from New York City, and like a lot of people from the Big Apple, headed south to Miami for the winter. Like many of those migrants, this car was ready for retirement, and it bottomed out with every major dip in the road. After a while, the scraping sound was like fingernails on a chalkboard, and we arrived at Pro Player Stadium none too soon.

Security met us at the entrance to the NFL Experience, and we were quickly led backstage to the VIP area. Although we were mobbed along the way, Bill instructed autograph seekers to walk with him, so he could accommodate their requests. We stopped many times for people to snap pictures of themselves or their children with Goldberg. When we finally arrived, Bill ran into Jerry Glanville, his former coach from the Falcons. He was there to introduce the Black Crowes, who just happened to be his neighbors back in Atlanta.

Jerry Glanville:

One night I went next door to complain about the loud music coming from their house, and I was thrilled to discover who my new neighbors were. They countered, "Hey, we don't come over to your house and complain about how you coach football!" After that, we became instant friends.

Coach Glanville wanted Bill and Scott to act as his bodyguards and escort him to the stage. After the introduction, we stayed for the concert. We hadn't been there thirty minutes, and we were all onstage with the Black Crowes. After we left the stage, Tom Arnold came up and introduced himself to Bill. "It's nice to see another member of the tribe do so well," he said, pulling down his shirt to reveal a Star of David tattooed on his chest.

Jerry Glanville holding court.

Because of the growing crowd around us, we were taken to the
NFL owners' VIP area. This was a rather stiff crowd, but we were
happy to have a little time to ourselves . . . or so we thought. From
this very conservative crowd came a steady stream of people
approaching Bill for his autograph. Boys, girls, adults, even NFL
players wanted to meet him. It was strange.

A well-dressed man approached our table and asked Bill if it
would be all right to make an introduction. "Sure," Bill said, and
another man in a suit came over and shook Bill's hand. "You'll be
wrestling in Madison on Wednesday," he said, "and I wanted to
meet you and welcome you to our state. I'm Tommy Thompson,
governor of Wisconsin."

**Me with
governor
Tommy
Thompson.**

This was getting better by the minute. Four security guards were assembled to take us to the stadium, and Bill called a buddy to try and get two extra tickets for Scott and his girl. He was offered only one, which would be left for Scott at the Will Call window. We were shuttled through the crowd again, and Bill continued to stop for pictures and autographs.

A couple of fans in their twenties yelled out, "Hey, Goldberg, keep up the good work! You take care of your fans and treat them right, not like the NFL guys we've seen today!" Bill thanked them and told them that he hadn't forgotten where he came from.

We stopped outside the entrance and summoned a security officer from inside the stadium. Scott and Bill were mobbed by fans when I recognized one of the all-time legends of football, and probably the greatest running back of all time. How ironic that at the biggest football game of the year, two professional wrestlers were surrounded by fans and Jim Brown walked into the stadium virtually unnoticed.

When the stadium official arrived, we explained that we were one ticket short. He motioned for us to follow him. With tickets in hand, we passed through the gate, and when Scott arrived, the guy moved the turnstile aside and let him pass around it. As luck would have it, the official's kids were wrestling fans, and Scott and Bill arranged to return the favor with pictures, and tickets for whenever they had a show in Miami.

A Florida highway patrolman observed our entrance and stopped us once we were inside. "Wait right here for a minute?" he asked. We thought we were busted, but he returned with a disposable camera—he wanted his picture taken with Bill!

We were finally escorted to our seats, and Bill thanked and dismissed the security people. They assured us that they would be nearby and would be there for us after the game. From the time that we sat down, people constantly approached Bill for autographs, and it was fun being at the Super Bowl and hearing fans call out, "Goldberg."

The Goldberg boys at play.

The couple behind us told Bill that he was their son's favorite sports hero. They asked if he would be so kind as to talk to him by phone at halftime. Bill agreed, but when he said hello, there was no response. The boy was too excited to talk!

"He has talked to the president of the United States at least twenty times," the boy's father said to Bill, "and he was too nervous to talk to you!" The man gave Bill his card, which substantiated his story. He was the national chairman of the Democratic Senate Selection Committee.

As the game wore on, and Atlanta fell further behind, more and more attention was directed toward Bill. "What could possibly happen next?" I asked my dad. It didn't take long to find out. A man came up to Bill and said, "I'm sorry for bothering you during the game, but would you please have your manager call me. We'd love to have you do some advertising for our company." He turned out to be the national marketing director for Miller Brewing Company. He returned to his seat three rows behind us, and I noticed that he was sitting with Richard Petty!

I walked upstairs with Mike and Bill to get a beer, and a man came up to us and introduced himself to Bill. He was wearing a NationsBank name tag, and Mike has done business with them for years. In fact, he had a meeting scheduled the following morning at NationsBank to discuss financing for a fleet of aircraft. A woman walked by, and the man stopped her and introduced Bill. Her kids were big fans, and she was thrilled to meet him, she said. She was introduced to Mike as the president of NationsBank.

"What branch do you run?" inquired Mike.

"Why, all of them," she explained. She was the president of the entire company! What a coincidence. Mike, as a sizable client, had always dealt with people in the upper echelon of the bank, and he had just met their boss through his younger brother.

The best is yet to come.

After we met the owners of a sporting-shoe company and a clothing company, a well-dressed woman came up to us who obviously knew Bill. She declared, with a smile and a Southern accent, "Why, Bill, it's so good to see you. I know that Taylor would love to come out and say hello, but he's kind of busy right now. I'm sure you understand."

But a few minutes later a man came up to us and shook Bill's hand enthusiastically. "Billy, I want to get one thing straight—I wasn't the one that released you, it was the director of player personnel! You were always one of my favorite players. I'm really proud of you, you've done real well for yourself."

It was Taylor Smith himself, and he was referring to an article in the *Atlanta Constitution* that quoted Bill as saying, "The luckiest day of my life was the day that Taylor Smith released me from the Falcons." The executive president and co-owner of the Atlanta Falcons left his seat when his team was driving for a score, to talk to Goldberg!

I just shook my head and ordered another beer.

We met up with Scott at the limo after the game, and he told us about his Super Bowl experience. He and his friend found an open skybox, and they just walked right in. They knew no one, but the people were happy to have him as their guest. Scott Steiner, with no airline ticket, no hotel room, and no ticket for the game, ended up flying in on a private jet, finding a hotel room three blocks from ours, and spending the game in a private skybox. He was happy that he hooked up with the Goldbergs.

Dad and Scotty—need I say more?

Minneapolis

Mike had business in Miami, so we were off to the land of ten thousand frozen lakes without him. The airlines were booked, but Jep Thornton was nice enough to arrange to have his plane pick us up Monday morning. When I lived in the Twin Cities, I'd visit Mike in Miami as often as possible to escape the brutal winters. I'd leave the frozen tundra and land in paradise, knowing that the opposite route was imminent. Invariably, I'd leave a beautiful day, only to descend through the clouds to the snow-covered land below. It would always be overcast, cold, and ugly when I returned, and the day after the Super Bowl was no exception.

We landed and set out to find a dress shirt with a twenty-two-inch neck. Finding a big-and-tall shop is no problem in the Twin Cities. There are plenty of overweight people to market to. I guess the "tall" makes people feel better about shopping there.

Fortunately, Bill didn't have to wrestle that night, he only had to do an interview in the ring with Mean Gene. Soon we were off to my restaurant, Dixies Calhoun, for dinner. The place was packed with fans anticipating his arrival, which is usually the case when Bill comes to town. We mixed with the crowd at the bar until it was time to eat.

A large group of us were seated for dinner, cordoned off from the crowd in the bar. Nature Boy Ric Flair was at one end of the table and Bill was at the other. In between, Mean Gene Okerlund was holding court with the twenty-odd guests.

"You're at the head of the table now, and that's just where you belong," shouted the Nature Boy to Goldberg. "It's your town, you're the man!" Ric surveyed the crowd and took a long draw from his cocktail. "This is what they don't teach you at the Power Plant," he said with a smile.

That night in Minneapolis was the end of a whirlwind four-day extravaganza that had taken us across the country and halfway back again. Tomorrow we would go our separate ways. Bill was headed to Washington, D.C., and I was going home to California. It was time to get a little sleep before our morning flights, and it was time for Bill and me to go our separate ways. It was really cool being able to spend so much time together, and I turned to Bill and said, "I'm very proud of you, Billy, you're all growed up now!"

"I love you, brother," he said. "The party is just beginning."

chapter ten

"I CHANGED GOLDBERG'S DIAPER"

by Jed Goldberg

If you've ever watched a professional wrestling match, you are no doubt familiar with the signs that many fans display throughout the matches. Generally, they proclaim their love or disdain for a certain wrestler. The above title is one, which I conceived but never had the nerve to display during my son's matches. No one would have believed me, anyway.

My son the wrestler has always been a person of surprises. First and foremost was the fact that he was actually born. As an obstetrician/gynecologist, I should have known better than to assume that the family was complete after the birth of our daughter twelve years prior. In 1966, I was a forty-two-year-old physician with a wife and three kids. Suddenly, incredibly, unexpectedly, it was my awkward duty to announce that there was going to be a fourth—and at the time, I could have used a fifth . . . of Scotch.

We gathered the family together and made the announcement of the impending event. This news was not received too favorably by the children, who probably didn't think that their parents still did such things. My oldest son, Mike, laughed hysterically; the younger son, Steve, stated that he was leaving home; and my daughter, Barbara, was joining him.

Bill's childhood was uneventful. He spent a considerable amount of time at his brothers' football and baseball games and his sister's horse shows. There were frequent "sandlot" football games in our front yard, and Bill soon began to play with the "big boys." As he grew older, he grew prodigiously, exceeding the height and weight of all of his teammates in Little League baseball. It became quite obvious that he was going to excel in sports, although wrestling was one he never attempted.

Bill played Little League, Pony League, and American Legion baseball. He was a moderately good pitcher and a powerful hitter, unless he was thrown a curveball. Unfortunately, he was whomp-eyed (an Okie-ism for a lens defect in one eye). Basketball provided comic relief. Bill was not fast, and his shooting was deficient, but he was a starter anyway. He was stationed under the basket and fed by his teammates for close-in shots, and very few high school players would challenge him. As a physician, I felt needed at the games, to attend to those who tried.

Bill began playing football in eighth grade. His height and weight, combined with his natural athletic skills, made him a fear-some competitor. In addition to playing on both the offensive and defensive lines, he learned another skill—as a kicker. Don "Babe" Chandler was a family friend. Babe had played with the Rams, the Giants, and had reached his zenith as the kicker and punter for Vince Lombardi's championship Green Bay Packers. Every summer, the Goldberg kids and their father would retrieve balls for Babe. In return, he acted as a kicking guru for Steve and then Bill, who went on to become a very good high school kicker and punter. That was at the time that kickers were converting to soccer style, but Bill refused to abandon his classic straight-on style.

Unbeknownst to me, Bill was hired as a bouncer at a local night-club. He was all of sixteen years old! The husband of one of my patients was a police officer, and one day he accosted me and told me about Bill's job, and also how dangerous he thought that it was: Regardless of Bill's strength, etc., it would not help against a knife or a gun. I most certainly agreed, and put a stop to this. At least that's what I thought at the time. I found out during the writing of this chapter that the owner of the club discovered Bill's true age after reading about his high school football prowess in the local newspaper. Bill was not dismissed, but was relegated to the parking lot, where he resumed his bouncer duties.

Although sports were a year-round activity, Bill found other interests, as well. He shared an interest in flying with his brothers and father. One day, as I was making a crucial landing, Bill was sitting on his brother (and my instructor) Mike's lap. Just as we cleared the threshold of the runway, Bill vomited all over Mike, making the landing doubly difficult for his old man. He never had time to acquire a license, but he frequently shared the controls with Mike and Steve.

What a goober.

Sailing and sailboat racing were also prominent activities during his youth. Big brother Mike had a large sailboat, in which we raced and cruised off Florida and the Caribbean. Key West was a favorite destination. At age sixteen, Bill won the arm-wrestling contest for our boat. We also had a pretty good tug-of-war team: Two of our crewmen were former pro footballers who later crewed on several America's Cup boats. Later in his sailing career, Bill was asked to sign on to one of the Cup contenders as a "grinder," winding huge winches to control the sails. Unfortunately, it would have interfered with his collegiate football career, so he turned it down.

By his junior year in high school, it was apparent that he was college football material. During his senior year, he was selected as the Lineman of the Year by *Tulsa World* and was named to the All-State team, sharing this distinction with his two brothers. At that time, I was the second father of three football All-Staters, sharing that honor with Mr. Selman—an interesting combination: a black and a Jew!

The frenzy of college recruiting began during the latter part of his junior year and continued in high gear throughout his senior year. Like his brothers before him, he wanted to attend college away from Oklahoma, although Barry Switzer almost had him convinced to sign as a Sooner. He returned from a visit to the University of Georgia and announced that he wanted to sign with the Bulldogs. I have often wondered what special inducements and circumstances he found in Athens—most likely it was in the person of Coach Vince Dooley, although, knowing Bill, it probably was the Georgia co-eds.

We were a typical jock family, attending Georgia games at home and away and, every year, a different Bowl game.

On one occasion, Mike and I traveled to Lexington, Kentucky, for the big SEC rivalry between the Bulldogs and the Wildcats. The home team upset the favored Bulldogs and the crowd was in a frenzy. We left our seats early and made our way to the visitors' locker room. Ahead of us were a knot of drunken Wildcat supporters, who began a tirade against the returning players. One particularly obnoxious fan began to make crude racist remarks about the Georgia players. Mike had had enough—he turned and smashed the bigot in the jaw, with a portable TV set. I tried to pull people off of Mike, when suddenly the crowd quieted. Bill, in full game regalia, had climbed the separating fence to protect his father and brother. The crowd melted away, and then several policemen appeared, who told us to get the hell out of there. Mike argued that he wouldn't leave until he could visit with his brother, but I—envisioning spending the night in a fit of claustrophobia in a cell—pushed him out of the crowd and to our rental car. For some reason, the Associated Press thought that this fracas was newsworthy, and put it on their national wire. When we went to Georgia the following week for the next game, the "Fighting Goldbergs" were famous!

I continued my treks to Bill's games, watching him with the Los Angeles Rams, the Sacramento Surge, and the Atlanta Falcons.

Injuries are a frequent complication of a sports career. Bill was a defensive lineman, and there were usually pile-ups after running plays. I would hold my breath until the unpiling, waiting to see if Bill would rise up from the bottom unscathed. He had been fairly fortunate during his college career, but that soon changed when he entered the pros. During the last preseason game with the Rams, he sustained a pulled hamstring. The defensive-line coach assured him after the game that he had made the final cut, but then the next day head coach John Robinson released him, because "they could not afford to carry an injured rookie." Although I am not usually a vindictive person, I prayed that the Rams would lose every game and that Robinson would be fired. Although they didn't lose every game, they lost more than they won, and Robinson *was* fired!

Speaking of being vindictive, how about this for a long memory: When Bill left the Rams, he was asked to sign with the Vancouver team of the Canadian Football League. When he was up in Canada checking out the team, he received a call from the Miami Dolphins, who asked that he come down for their evaluation. Bill flew to Miami, and after a cursory look, he was informed that he was too small to play defensive lineman for the Dolphins. Fast-forward to February 2000. Bill was in Miami as a guest of the Miami Heat NBA basketball team. During a time-out, he joined in throwing T-shirts to the crowd. Spotting the former Dolphin coach Don Shula sitting in the audience, he strode up to him, shoved a T-shirt in his lap, and said, "Thanks, Coach, for not signing me," and went back to his floor-side seat.

Bill's last and worst football injury occurred in a Falcons game, and then, suddenly, there was no more football.

When Bill was twelve years old, he was subjected to the trauma of the separation and divorce of his parents. Like so many children of today, he felt the strains and divided loyalty that go along with such an event, living with his mother during the week and with me on weekends and during the summer. I am sure that there are scars that will always be present as a result of the parental rift.

My second marriage turned out to be a disaster, and it was obvious one night that it was all over. As Bill and I left, my erstwhile wife celebrated our departure with a well-chosen statement: "There go the Beverly Hillbillies!"

Bill was a wonderful companion during this stressful period, even though he almost ate me out of house and home. Every morning I fixed him bacon and eggs—ten eggs at a serving! I hope that his arteries have recovered from the shock. On another occasion, we were sailboat racing in Newport, Rhode Island, when I had a heart attack. I was in the hospital for several days, and Bill

An imposing pitcher.

stayed with me the whole time, then he accompanied me back to Tulsa, and stayed at my side through my second heart operation. These experiences built a bond between us that I will always cherish.

I've done a number of interviews just because I am Bill Goldberg's father. The most frequently asked question is "What was your reaction when Bill said that he was going to be a wrestler?" Before I give the answer to that question, I have to set the background. First of all, as you already know if you're reading this, Bill was in a state of occupational limbo. After realizing that football was no longer an option, he vacillated among personal trainer; salesman for a nutritional-drug company, then a beer company; and several other jobs of that ilk. He was staying in shape through regular attendance at local Atlanta gyms, and had met several professional wrestlers.

My background in wrestling was almost zilch; I had once been drafted by the high school wrestling coach to work out with one of my football teammates, whose only wrestling knowledge had been obtained at Monday night professional bouts at the Tulsa Coliseum. He picked me up and threw me against the gym wall—that was it for wrestling and me!

As for professional wrestling, I recall seeing a mustachioed, bald-headed short guy with a mike interviewing one or two pre-Neanderthal types whose vocal style was screaming at the top of their lungs. I also remember Gorgeous George on black-and-white TV. I had met Cowboy Bill Watts, who lived in Tulsa and whose son played football in high school at the same time as Bill. In addition to these faint memories, my oldest son, Mike, had roomed in Minneapolis with two wrestling luminaries: Ric Flair and Ken Patera.

Bill called me one evening and broached the idea of becoming a professional wrestler. I must confess that I was taken aback by the thought. What was the future in such a career? Could you make a decent living? What would I tell my friends? If I sounded less than accepting of such a role for Bill, that was probably the case. I did *not,* as alleged by some, hang up on him! I did know that he would work his tail off to be a success, whatever success meant in professional wrestling.

So, now he is a famous professional wrestler. What of my trepidations about such a career? Barring injury, he could wrestle for many years. As for income, he makes more than I did in thirty-five years of medical practice. He is a recognized celebrity, and may have a future in the movies. As far as my friends are concerned, I am also a recognized celebrity, a VIP: BILL GOLDBERG'S FATHER. Although I sometimes miss my former identity as a godlike physician, I don't begrudge one second of the reflected fame I enjoy. The number of Goldberg followers there are continually amazes me. These include not only the usual devotees, but also a great number of "closet" wrestling fans, including professionals—such as my urologist and cardiologist, waiters and maître d's, painters, plumbers, etc. It gives me the opportunity to get better service by offering in return a signed picture of my son the wrestler!

During my early years as a high school football official, I used to take Bill with me to out-of-town games. Little did I know that instead of watching his old man throw yellow handkerchiefs, he was trying to romance high school girls—at the tender age of eleven! Although I never thought of him as a Romeo, he did come up with some beauties. Several of my patients turned out to be old girlfriends of his—as did numerous e-mailers and phone-callers, who wanted his phone number after he became famous. It is amazing how many long-lost girlfriends, cousins, and high school buddies have emerged from the woodwork. Most of them want freebies to the wrestling shows; some want to be able to go backstage and see Bill; others have diverse motives, at which one can only hazard a guess.

Who Is Bill?

Most of us have a multifaceted personality to some degree, with normal temperament swings. People in the entertainment business frequently have "onstage" and "at home" faces. As GOLDBERG! Bill is a huge, somewhat brutish person who speaks in husky high-volume tones. For most of his career, he has been a "face," a good guy, fighting evil. None of this, however, is expressed by his performance in the ring as he first intimidates and then destroys his opponents. Many of his followers feel that he would make a perfect "heel," or bad guy, and they are probably correct. He even looks menacing and mean.

Out of the ring, he is a pussycat. I have never seen or heard of him refusing to stop, talk, and give an autograph to any reasonable fan, especially children. He visits children's hospitals wherever he is performing. He gives many days a year to charitable events involving children, especially those who are seriously or mortally ill. He has been the recipient of many requests by the Make-A-Wish Foundation and others, such as the foundation in Aspen, Colorado, headed by the former tennis great Andrea Jaeger.

His other great cause is working with the Humane Society of the United States. This, again, is a labor of love. One of my proudest moments as a father was to be present in Washington when he represented this organization before a House committee. He even wore a coat and tie!

"Jewish wrestler" is as oxymoronic as "fresh frozen jumbo shrimp." I cannot speak for Bill as to his theological beliefs, but I feel certain that he has some religious feelings, whatever they may be. He studied for and went through the ancient rite of Bar Mitzvah as a thirteen-year-old. That, however, was his last touch with formal Judaism, although he has always considered himself Jewish (difficult to deny, with a name like Goldberg).

Father and son.

Early in his career, considering the use of his name as his wrestling moniker, Bill confided that he had some qualms about appearing in his underwear before predominantly Southern and Baptist audiences. To this date, there have been no open negative reactions from the wrestling world—certainly a credit not only to Bill but to the majority of the fans. To my knowledge, he never ran into overt anti-Semitism; but then again, who in his right mind would want to insult him to his face?

During his high school and college days, he felt that if he didn't play on Yom Kippur, the most holy Jewish holiday, he would be letting his team down. Prior to the Georgia-Florida game in Jacksonville, he and a Jewish lineman from Florida were both roundly criticized from the pulpit by the rabbi in Jacksonville, because they chose to play on this day. For the record, however, he will not wrestle on Yom Kippur.

He has been the subject of adulation by so many Jewish groups and journalists that I know that he feels this is a responsibility he is willing to accept as a representative of his coreligionists. The fact that he chose to be known by his last name speaks to that feeling. When it was decided that "Goldberg" would be the wrestling name, it was suggested that he wear a Star of David on his trunks. He vetoed the idea: if the name itself didn't paint the picture, why flaunt religion? By the way, most people think that former heavyweight boxing champion Max Baer was Jewish, because he wore the emblem on his trunks. Not true! That was strictly a marketing ploy designed to attract the considerable New York Jewish boxing fans. In essence, Bill is a professional wrestler who happens also to be Jewish.

I can only answer the question "Who is Bill?" as his father. He is a damn fine son, who, for the most part, has kept a level head in

Doc Goldberg and his boys.

spite of his success. Offstage, he is a "gentle giant." Lest the reader think that he is a perfect gentleman, I cite his rotten temper, a gift from me, and a chronic inability to keep to a schedule. The bottom line, however, is that I am proud to be his father, and I know that we will always maintain the strong bond between us.

chapter eleven

GROWING UP GOLDBERG

My grandfather worked for the circus. My other grandfather was the biggest auctioneer in the South. So I guess being an entertainer is in my blood.

I was born December 27, 1966. My parents named me William Scott—William after my grandfather Willie, and Scott after "Shit, I don't know." The "Shit, I don't know" part is a direct quote from my father, Jed, whose real name is Judell. What a switch for him, changing from his totally ethnic name to one most associated with a hillbilly. Jed was definitely a more appropriate handle for growing up in Oklahoma. My mother's name is Ethel, and so was my paternal grandmother's. My family had the Ethel Goldberg market cornered in Tulsa, Oklahoma, where I grew up. My mother began playing the violin when she was four, and went on to become a concert violinist. When she started having kids, she hung up her bow . . . but not the arrows. My mom raised orchids, and she is an international orchid judge. She named one of her prized orchids after me: the Spotted Phalaenopsis Bill Goldberg.

PHAL: BILL GOLDBERG

My father was an obstetrician/gynecologist, and was a pretty good family planner, until I came along. My oldest brother is Mike, followed by Steve three years and one month later, and Barbara, three years and one month after that. I came along twelve years later.

Since my dad was a doctor, we lived pretty well, and because I was accident prone, it was convenient having him around. Once he sewed up my forehead in the middle of the living room, and another time he sutured a laceration on the top of my head, in the library. One of my scars was from a baseball bat and the one on my head was from a statue of a clown that one of my dad's patients gave him. It was on top of an armoire that I wanted to climb, and the statue fell on top of me and stuck in my head. I should have known where my life was headed after that early run-in with the clown. I got used to stitches at an early age.

Like many kids of my generation, I didn't grow up in the stereo-typical good ol' American family that my brothers and sister did. In a lot of ways, it was quite the opposite. My parents were divorced, and I got into my fair share of trouble. But as bad as it may have been at times, it sure as hell could have been a lot worse.

Ever since I was a little kid, all I wanted to do was become a professional football player. My earliest memories are of being involved with sports and of going on trips with the family, and that's about it. I wanted to be like my brothers and play football. I remember kicking footballs with Steve, and watching him and Mike play in college. I used to go to a lot of high school football games with my dad when he was an official. Traitor. I traveled with him throughout the state of Oklahoma, and that's when I actually started liking girls. I met a lot of girls that way. I'd tell them, "Yeah, my dad's the umpire." Whatever.

The most vivid memory of my childhood was of my parents' divorce and my being the pawn in between them. Whether they realized it or not, whether it was intentional or not, I was the knot in their tug-of-war rope. And a lot of the memories I have are centered around being strangled by that rope.

I divided time between my parents' houses, and certain times when I did cool things with my dad, my mom would find out and try to top them. Seemingly, they were trying to compete with each other. I got away with a lot as a kid because I followed in my brothers' and sister's footsteps. They had broken my parents in for me. Mom and Dad knew everything that they had pulled, so most of what I was about to do to them had already been done. I don't know whether it lessened the blow to them and numbed the effect or whether I was as keen and swift as I thought I was. I got away with my share of things, and I'd like to think at least some of them were new and unique.

My next-door neighbor Charlie Downs was my best friend for years. I met him the day we moved into the neighborhood. We did some goofy shit . . . like the time we taped skateboards to our feet and tried to jump the creek. We built a ramp and we needed the tape to hold the skateboard to our feet while airborne. Bad idea. Another time, we decided to build a go-cart, and we kept adding stuff to it until it ended up the size of a car. It never made it out of the garage. After that, I knew that I wasn't mechanically inclined.

Charlie and I got in a lot of trouble. Once my dad caught us smoking cigarettes up in the carport, and to teach us a lesson, he made us smoke, like, three packs apiece. They were Kool menthols, and it was brutal. After that, I hated my mother for smoking them.

I remember one time going over a jump on my bicycle. I flew up in the air and I landed hard . . . right on the head of my Johnson. Not that my dick was so long that I ran over it. I jammed it into the seat when the bike hit the ground. I thought it got cut off or something. I think I was eight at the time. Fortunately, I had a helmet.

Every Saturday I would spend the night at my grandmother's house, just as my brothers and sister had done years before. Grandfather Willie passed away before I was born, and the Saturday nights I spent with Grammy Ethel were the highlight of her week. She was born in Minsk, Russia, and she immigrated to America with her father when she was three. It was at her house that I watched my first professional wrestling match. It was before cable TV, and the programming options were limited, to say the least. There were only three channels, and the choices were *The Lawrence Welk Show, Bonanza,* or *Texas Championship Wrestling.* Wrestling won by default, because it most resembled sports. I also remember watching Mid-South wrestling in Tulsa, which was run by Cowboy Bill Watts. The promoter was named LeRoy McGuirk, and my sister, Barbara, went to school with LeRoy's daughter, Kathleen. LeRoy was blind, and he would have made an excellent referee. I wasn't an avid fan, there just wasn't much else to watch.

I would sit in Grammy's swivel chair and watch Fritz Von Erich, Ivan Putski, Andre the Giant, Mil Mascaras, and Bruiser Brody. Grammy would keep a steady flow of food coming my way, and I would typically down five to ten bacon-and-egg sandwiches and a

With my grandmother Ethel.

couple of root-beer floats. I remember how the room and the chair used to smell even now . . . before and after the sandwiches. I'd wake up in the morning and eat matzo and eggs, and when I was fourteen, Grammy let me drive her '62 T-bird to the grocery store. The same car is now sitting in Steve's garage in California, still in pristine condition.

Barbara would come over for a while before going out for the night. When Grammy started going sideways, she began talking to the TV, and she thought that the people on TV were talking back to her. This went on even after programming ended for the night, and she would continue her conversations with the test-pattern Indian. She also had some lengthy conversations with television snow. I'd wake up in the middle of the night and freak out from Grammy ranting and raving at the tube. I was just a kid, and I didn't understand what was going on. I loved Grammy tremendously, and even though she's long since left this planet, I still go by her house whenever I'm in Tulsa.

The First Time I Used a Foreign Object

Grammy Ethel had Alzheimer's disease, and I remember one of my so-called friends playing a cruel trick on her. He went up to her door and said that he was me and that I wasn't coming over that weekend. When I found out what he did, I invited him over to our house, and being a good host, I offered him milk and cookies. I returned from the kitchen with the snack, and little did he know that I had pissed in about half of his glass of milk. I watched him drink the whole thing, and when he finished, out of nowhere I smashed him over the head with a frying pan. I think the door hit him in the ass on the way out.

Grandfather Willie worked for the Sells-Flotow circus before taking up a more respectable career owning a pawnshop and then a jewelry store. While with the circus, he sold tickets, put up the tents, cleaned up after the elephants, and did whatever else was needed.

My father tells a story about when he was a kid and his dad took him to the circus. They went to see the sideshows, and the fat lady, "Alice from Dallas," came up to Willie and asked if Jed was his son. Willie introduced the two, and Alice gave my dad a big hug, which totally engulfed him, almost smothering him with her dripping layers of lard. From that day on, my father has avoided the circus.

Steve, Mike, Barbara, and me.

My Great-grandfather the Professional Wrestler

My other grandmother's name was Rene, and her maiden name was Wolfson. Her father's name (my great-grandfather) was Morris, and he emigrated from Russia. Morris was only five foot nine, but he was a big man for the times. He moved to St. Louis, and when times were slow in the peddling business, he actually wrestled for money. He got in the ring with a famous wrestler named Frank Gotch, and was paid for grappling with him—which, technically, made him a professional wrestler. He eventually moved to Jacksonville, Florida, and became quite a successful businessman.

Grandmother Rene was born in Baltimore and grew up in Jacksonville. That's where she met my grandfather, Marcel Kasner, who literally whisked her out of town in the middle of the night. Her parents didn't care too much for Marcel, and my grandparents loaded up the car, tied a mattress to the roof, and headed west.

Pop . . . A Very Rare Man
Morris David Wolfson
1879–1948

Poverty stalked the young Wolfson family of four, so Morris worked at any odd jobs he could find. Physically, "Pop," as he was later called, was extremely powerful, though standing only 5' 9". Going from one gym to another, earning a little money for his family, Pop was paid to wrestle with the great American Freestyle Champion, Frank Gotch. He'd never wrestled before, but stories are that he held his own in the ring, and that was really something in those days.

An excerpt from the biography of my great grandfather, Morris Wolfson.

Marcel was six foot seven—or five foot nineteen, as he used to tell people. He wore size fifteen shoes, and he was from the old country. He came over alone from Bucharest, Romania, when he was thirteen, and landed at Ellis Island. During World War II the Nazis sent many of his family members who stayed in Romania to concentration camps, and killed them, because they were Jewish.

Marcel was a traveling auctioneer in the South, and then he became a true Okie when he ran out of money on his way out west. He was quite a character, and he billed himself as the biggest auctioneer in the South, and then the biggest jeweler in Oklahoma. At five foot nineteen, he probably was.

The biggest auctioneer in the South, my grandfather, Marcel Kasner.

I had a pretty good childhood. Mike went off to college the year after I was born; Steve was around until I was three. I spent the most time growing up with Barbara. She went off to college when I was six, but she came back to Tulsa after she graduated. I always looked up to my brothers because of athletics, and it sucked that they were so much older. I didn't have the benefit of having them around in school with me, to hang out with and learn from. I had to learn on my own.

My dad took up sailing, and we spent a lot of time on Grand Lake o' the Cherokees, Lake Keystone, and Lake Yahola. I remember a sailing vacation to the Bahamas. Everyone went except Mom, who didn't care too much for being on the water. Maybe that's why Dad always had a boat. We chartered a sailboat and sailed around the islands, and that's when I learned to scuba dive and drink Heineken beer. We were told of shark sightings; it was really fun, because I was with my father, brothers, and sister, sailing around the Bermuda Triangle. Steve brought along a Zap comic book entitled *Captain Piss Gums and the Dyke Pirates,* and when I returned home and Mom asked about the trip, I quoted the good captain, and told her to "bite me crank, matey."

When Barbara graduated from college, she moved back home, until my father split and advised her to do the same. That's when the proverbial shit hit the fan and spattered all over Barbara and me. It was like World War III, and I was in the no-man's-land. To make matters worse, someone poisoned my two dogs, and the one that survived went to live with Barbara.

I think *the neighbors* did it. I couldn't stand our neighbors, and one day I invited a couple of the kids over and told them that the dogs were penned up. I was hoping that the dogs would eat them, because to say I didn't like them is an understatement. The dogs chased them, but the kids were able to jump over the fence in time to save their hides. Unfortunately, they were fast enough to escape.

I was really grateful to have Barbara around when I was growing up. We lived in a very competitive household, and she was the only one who didn't play football. This was due to circumstances beyond her control—she was born female. Barbara rode horses and competed in numerous horse shows. I remember one time she put me in one of the shows, too. I was part of the intermission, a "costume class." I was seven or eight years old. I was on her horse, Gooch, and I was dressed up like a cowboy, even though I was riding on an English saddle. The crowd was watching me, and I was so proud that I felt compelled to pull out my guns—my cap guns—and start shooting them in the air. The next thing I knew, Gooch took off and started bucking, and I became Bronco Billy Goldberg. Barb ran out and grabbed her horse's reins, and saved me from taking my first bump.

Barbara wanted me to have the same childhood she and my brothers enjoyed. But that was impossible, since I was twelve years younger, and Mom and Dad had been there, done that. So she attempted to create a better world for me. She took me *everywhere* with her, even when she had something better to do. I distinctly remember each Fourth of July. My parents had little desire to shoot off fireworks (except at each other), so they gave Barbara some money, and we would buy enough "ammo" to last us a lifetime.

Bite me crank, matey!

Barb used to take me to Tulsa Oiler baseball games. They were the American Association farm club for the St. Louis Cardinals and I think her motive was to check out the guys. Mine was to collect autographs, and I used to beg to stay after the game, and she always complied. The players were usually very accommodating, including

Keith Hernandez, who made it to the big leagues and had a great career, first with the Cardinals and then with the Mets. Maybe those players' actions were a prelude to the way I deal with the public now. I'm rarely too busy to sign an autograph.

Barbara went off to Stephens College, in Columbia, Missouri. Stephens was an all-girls school, and when I was eight years old I had the pleasure of staying overnight with Barb in her dorm. There were girls walking around in their underwear, not paying any attention to me. I, on the other hand, paid a lot of attention to them, and I think that was a pivotal time in my attraction to girls.

Barbara helped me out a lot, and if it weren't for her I'd have gone insane. I share her love of animals and for the holidays. Barb and her boyfriend Larry (now her husband), bought me and Mom a rottweiler puppy. I named him Rocky after the tenacious palooka in the movie. This was my first dog, and he became my best friend. He eventually went to college with me, and ended up living out his days on a farm owned by one of my professors.

Rocky and I ran away together about twenty thousand times. I'd get upset for one reason or another, and I would bolt. We ran away as far as Mom would let us go and when she'd catch up to us she'd utter her usual threat. I'd be running down the street with Rocky at my side, Mom would pull up next to us in the car and say, "If you don't stop, I'm going to throw myself in front of the car." I'd say, "O.K., go ahead, I just don't see how you're going to do it." She was going to throw herself in front of the car she was driving, but somehow I must have believed that she could do it, because it always made me turn around.

When my parents split up, I lived with my mom most of the time. Mealtime was always an adventure. Mom was infamous for her dinners. She was great cooking for the family when the rest of the kids were growing up, but she must not have been too inspired to cook for just the two of us. She'd just pull something out of the freezer, which was stuffed full of a variety of iced-over foods. From the freezer she'd put it into the oven, and when it came out, it would look fine and dandy on the outside, but inside it was hard as an iceberg. Here is a recount of a typical dinner:

1. *Remove steak from freezer, place in oven. Cook until almost thawed, and place on a dinner plate and serve.*
2. *Remove steak from plate, and place into watering mouth of waiting dog, Rocky.*
3. *Go out with friends and eat fast food.*

Mom wondered why I was eating out all the time, and why Rocky was 130 pounds.

When I was growing up, I was afforded a lot of opportunities, thanks to Mike and Steve. Aside from watching wrestling at my grandmother's house when I was a kid, the only other experience I had with professional wrestling was through my brothers. Mike and Steve played football for the University of Minnesota, and my parents would occasionally take me along to their games. Mike shared a house in Minneapolis for a while with Ric Flair and Ken Patera. Ric went on to become the Nature Boy and Ken went on to become an Olympic heavyweight weight lifter. Later, in his wrestling career, Patera formed a tag team with Mr. Saito. Together, out of the ring, they teamed up on a female deputy sheriff in Wisconsin, and were sent to prison for beating her up. Mr. Saito was further immortalized by having a drink named after him.

THE MR. SAITO Over ice, pour equal shots of Bailey's Irish Cream and Rumplemintz into a cocktail shaker. Shake like a deputy, and strain into a shot glass.

Former roommates, Nature Boy and Mike.

Steve was teammates in college with Scott Irwin—who later became one of the Long Riders with his brother Wild Bill—and Jim Brunzell, who became Jumping Jim Brunzell of the Killer Bees. And when Steve went on to the bar and restaurant business, one of his favorite customers was, and still is, the legendary Mean Gene Okerlund.

I was frequently subjected to some pretty crazy people while hanging around my brothers, especially Homer and Gundy. Gary Holmes, A.K.A. Homer, was Mike's best friend. Homer's ambition growing up was to be a millionaire by the time he was sixteen. He was bummed because he missed his goal by three years. He was a big Norwegian with gigantic calves and huge balls—literally, I've been told. In college at the University of Minnesota, he grew tired of school, so he found a way to beat the system. He dressed up in a white coat, grabbed a briefcase, and sauntered into the administration building, where he proceeded to change his transcript. He passed himself off as a computer programmer, and he gave himself passing grades on his toughest remaining classes.

Jeff Gunderson, A.K.A. Gundy, is one of the craziest guys I've ever known. He was a teammate of Steve's, and his best friend. Gundy once bit a guy's ear off in a fight. Now he could sew it back on, since he's an emergency-room physician.

When I was sixteen years old, I was lucky enough to accompany my brothers and Homer and Gundy to Super Bowl XVII in Pasadena. The night before the game, we went out for some serious partying, and I ended up riding with Gundy to the next watering hole. He made an illegal U-turn over the center median, right in front of one of L.A.'s finest. The policeman pulled us over, and Gundy pleaded with him not to throw him in jail. He told the officer that he worked in the emergency room nearby, and that someday he might have to provide medical services to him or one of his fellow officers. The guy handcuffed Gundy to a chain-link fence and called the emergency room to verify his employment there.

After waiting for us for a while, Mike, Steve, and Homer retraced their steps and found us in the parking lot, with Gundy still shackled to the fence. His story checked out, and the officer let us go, under the condition that Gundy wouldn't drive. This was a typical trip with my older brothers, and I guess I can blame them for my early evil ways. Incidentally, it was a great game. The Washington Redskins beat the Miami Dolphins, and John Riggins carried the ball, like, five hundred times.

Growing up, I was very lucky to have Mike as an older brother, because not only was he a great person, he was a very successful businessman who loved to spend his money on cool things. He had sailboats and airplanes, and he was very generous. Thanks to him, I've flown a T-34 Mentor military trainer, a glider, and the Goodyear Blimp. I've been at the helm of his fifty-one-foot Swan sailboat, and partied throughout the Caribbean with his wild crew of friends. Michael has opened my eyes to many things, to say the least.

Once we sailed to Key West in the annual Fort Lauderdale to Key West race. During one of the daily races, I was somehow left in the care of none other than Jeff Gunderson. Gundy promised to keep a close watch over me, but when everyone returned to the designated meeting place, I was nowhere to be found. And neither was Gundy, because he had gone in search of a mate of the opposite sex. I was left at the Mount Gay tent, where I helped myself to more than my fair share of rum—which should have been none, since I was, like, twelve at the time. Incidentally, if there ever was a Mount Gay, Key West was the right place for it.

By the time Mike and my dad found me, I was three-plus sheets to the wind, and they were none too happy with me . . . or Gundy. I had to stick around the hotel the next day, which was fine with me, since there was a topless beach on the property.

Steve provided his own brand of entertainment, since he and Homer owned the premier college bar at the University of Minnesota. It wasn't too bad hanging around checking out the scenery while eating everything on the menu. I was in heaven. In fact, I still do the same thing in his restaurants in the Twin Cities and San Diego.

School

Growing up in Tulsa, Oklahoma, I went to Eisenhower and Elliot elementary schools consecutively, and I went to Edison Junior and Senior High. I remember getting paddled quite frequently at Elliot. This was when it was O.K. for teachers to discipline their students, which would be much too dangerous for them to do in today's society.

One of the many times I got spanked in school was when I got into a fight with Bill Morris, god rest his soul. Bill and I were going to meet after school and duke it out, for some reason I can't recall. We talked about it so much during the day that by the time school ended, we really didn't want to fight. We planned it out that we'd just wing it, kind of like what I do today.

When it got out of hand, and he started hitting me for real, I started hitting him back. The gym teacher came and broke it up, and paddled us both. I knew him from class, and we were pretty friendly, so when he finished, I thanked him.

I was pretty defiant in high school. I wasn't known to attend classes regularly, and this was evidenced by the fact that I wasn't in too many yearbook pictures. That was an easy day to skip, but it was difficult explaining to my mom why they forgot to include my picture.

I was kind of a loner in high school. I stayed away from the crowd, even though I was a fairly decent sports figure. I wasn't a social butterfly, like most of the cool people in my school and neighborhood at the time. I always walked to the beat of a different drummer. I was friendly with a lot of people, but I wasn't necessarily friends with them.

I have vivid memories of throwing parties when Mom was out of town. I remember one time she came back early, and people were passed out all around the house and scattered all about the yard. She didn't seem mad though, because she was dancing in the living room with my friends. Then she danced her way into the bathroom, where I was dancing my head into the toilet. This seemed to amuse her, which at the time was no comfort to me.

My mom crashing my parties was a common occurrence throughout my high school years. But let's face it, when your mom joins the party how bad can your punishment be?

Ethel Goldberg:

Billy showed quite an interest in my orchids, and he frequently took his friends into my greenhouse. I thought that he was showing them my orchids, until I discovered some strange weedlike plants growing in between the shelves.

Bill was a mischievous kid, to say the least. He was a handful, and I always tried to stay one step ahead of him. I was on a first-name basis with his principal in elementary school.

My Name Is Goldberg, and Yes, I'm a Jew

In fact, my whole family is Jewish, but it's no big deal to me. I don't stand in the middle of the ring after a match and thank Moses for my victory, like so many athletes today thank their Lord. My grandfathers were both Jew-lers, which I thought was carrying their religion a bit too far.

Growing up, I always wanted a Christmas tree, and finally one year Barb bought me a Hanukkah bush. We proudly displayed it in our front window, until the cantor from the temple drove by and mistook it for a Christmas tree. I went to Hebrew school and Sunday school, and I remember that I didn't like it too much. It wasn't that I didn't like being Jewish, it's just that I didn't like being in another type of school, especially one that didn't have an athletic program.

I remember one time specifically that I didn't want to go to Hebrew school. I was lying in my parents' bed, and I convinced my mom that I was sick and I couldn't go to school. My dad came in and said, "That's cool, you can stay home." He turned around and started walking out of the room, then he stopped suddenly and said, "Do you want to go bowling?" and I said, "Yeah!" BUSTED. I remember trying to get out of a lot of religious obligations.

At thirteen, I had my Bar Mitzvah, and I remember drinking a lot of wine and getting a lot of gifts, and I remember that I was glad when it was over. Being Jewish meant that kids made fun of me every once in a while. The turning point came when I finally had to crank a kid at the 7-Eleven for making fun of my religion. I took his insults until finally I exploded, and I turned into Goldberg. I'll leave what happened next to your imagination.

Mac and Don and the Caravan

My first job was at McDonald's. I always loved to eat, and I was in hog heaven being around so much food. When burgers and fries sat out too long, it was company policy to throw them out, which seemed criminal to me. I took it upon myself to eat as much of this "old" food as possible, and when the manager found out, I was given my walking papers and sent down the road.

I was sixteen at the time, and I was staying with my recently divorced and remarried father, in his new wife's house. Every day that I had to stay with them really sucked. It was very evident that she wanted nothing to do with me, and I felt the same way about her.

A couple of dabs of my father's cologne led to their ultimate demise. I was walking out the door to go on a date, and as I passed her, she caught a whiff of my scent. She went ballistic. "I bought that cologne for your dad, not for you!" she screamed. "I'm tired of living with the Beverly Hillbillies!" I hightailed it out the door, never to return.

Later that evening, I called to check in with my dad. He had been upstairs and heard her yelling at me. He apologized, and asked me if I could come pick him up, because we were getting the hell out of there. We moved into the Residence Inn that night, and I was very happy to be away from that woman. From that day on, I was determined to make something out of my life, and even though my dad's name was Jed, I would not grow up to be Beverly Hill-Billy Goldberg.

Although I was only a short-timer at McDonald's, I still saved up enough money to get a car, with a little help. It was a Pontiac Trans Am, and I paid twelve hundred dollars for it. My dad had agreed to split the cost with me. I paid two hundred, and he paid a grand. The car turned out to be stolen, by the way.

Later that year, I went to work as a bouncer at the Caravan Ballroom. I lied about my age, and I got away with it because of my size. One day the owner was reading the *Tulsa Tribune,* and he came upon the All-City high school football preview. There was his new bouncer staring back at him from the page, a top junior prospect for Edison High.

He called me into the office, and when I saw the paper on his desk, I was sure that he was going to fire me on the spot. Instead, he took pity on me and relegated me to the parking lot, where my duties included cleaning up beer bottles and trash and beating people up if they were out of line.

Sports

All of the Goldberg boys played sports, and I'm proud to say we were all pretty good. My dad played football in high school and then played fullback and linebacker for Johns Hopkins. When he joined the Navy during World War II, he played guard both ways for Harvard, and he was honorable mention All–New England. Football actually saved him from going overseas when he failed a quantitative analysis class. He could have been called to active duty, but because he was a standout player, they wanted him to stay on the team. He was ordered to retake the class and get no lower than a B. He passed and stayed out of the war, and finished college and then medical school.

Both Mike and Steve played football and baseball in high school. They were both All-Conference, All-City, and All-State in football at Edison, and I followed in their footsteps, earning the same hon-

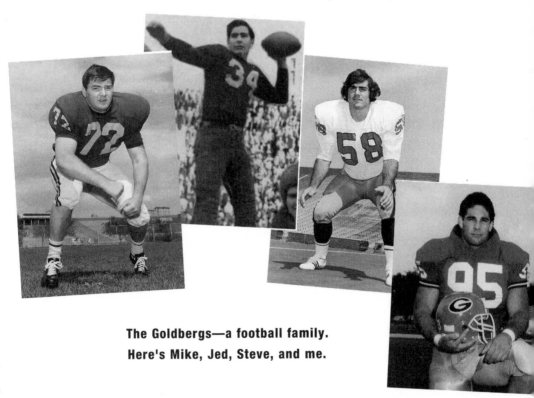

**The Goldbergs—a football family.
Here's Mike, Jed, Steve, and me.**

ors at the same high school. Both of them attended the University of Minnesota on football scholarships. Mike played defensive tackle, and Steve played linebacker and was the placekicker. Mike started for two years and was offered a tryout with the New York Giants after college. He smartly declined, having been offered an opportunity to enter the airplane business. Flying surpassed football as his priority in life, and he has been very successful in the aviation business ever since.

Steve injured his back, and although he was unable to continue playing linebacker, he kept on kicking. He was one of the last of the straight-on kickers, and he held most of the kicking records at the U. of M. He kicked a fifty-two-yard field goal against Ohio State, and he signed with the Oakland Raiders after college. After George Blanda came out of retirement, Steve was released, and he had very short stints with a couple of teams in the World Football League. The following year, he signed with the Vikings, and lasted all of seven days before hanging up his square-toed shoe. Having an affinity for eating and drinking, Steve entered the restaurant business, and I can still count on him for a hot meal and a cold beer.

My sporting career began at an early age, although my parents wouldn't let me play organized football until the eighth grade. At various times I was on the tennis team, the bowling team, and the diving team. I was once a ball boy during a match with Ilie Nastase and Vitas Gerulaitis . . . I think.

I started playing baseball in grade school, and my dad would get quite intense at my games. I remember one game when I was pitching and he almost got into a fight with my friend Adam Singer's dad. Mr. Singer was the manager and third-base coach, and he kept yelling at me because of my poor pitching performance. Jed couldn't take the criticism, and ripped off his jacket and went after Mr. Singer. Adam and I were watching in disbelief as our dads were standing there yelling at each other. Another time when I was pitching, Dad got real pissed off because the umpire wasn't calling strikes. He was furious, and he stormed off to the parking lot and his car.

My father was an amateur radio operator, and he went to his car to cool off and check the weather using his handheld ham-radio transceiver. The umpire got nervous because he thought that my dad's radio was a gun, and he called the police. Two squad cars showed up, and the ump looked like a chump.

I was reclusive and I hid in sports. I played football, baseball, and basketball in high school. The only thing I want to say about my basketball career is that I couldn't shoot very well, so I just stood under the basket to retrieve rebounds and shoot layups. More than once, my dad had to come out of the stands to give medical attention to opponents who got in my way. Oh, and white men can't jump, especially this one.

My plan was to get out of Tulsa by playing football. I always knew I would—I wasn't cocky, I just knew. My two brothers had done that, and I was next. It was my destiny. I wanted to follow in their footsteps and become the third Goldberg to go out of state on scholarship and be a success.

I was pretty good, and I played both ways. I remember the last time I played a skill position. I was tight end, and the ball was thrown to me. It hit me in the face mask, and of course I missed it. That was the last pass ever thrown to me. I remember punting and kicking and following in Steve's footsteps . . . literally. I wore the famous punter and kickoff specialist Ray Guy's kicking shoe, which Steve took as a souvenir when he was cut by the Raiders. It was a size ten and I stuffed my size thirteen foot in it. I went to various kicking camps throughout the country. One at Auburn, one at Penn State, and one in River Falls, Wisconsin. I remember kicking a field goal to win the city championship against a rival high school from the other side of town. When I was walking back to the car with Mom, a couple of guys walking behind us were talking about stabbing me. Mind you, I was in the eighth grade. Tulsa, Oklahoma, what a place. They take their football seriously down there.

My escapades as a kicker were plentiful. During one rainy game, the field became sloppy, and when I punted, I pulled a real-life

Charlie Brown. The ball went about forty yards into the air and four yards behind me. Another time when the ball was snapped over my head, I chased it down, retrieved it, and headed to the sideline. There was only one player between me and turning the corner. From what I remember, he was like three feet tall. Needless to say, he was the smallest person on their team, including the ball boy. I didn't pay too much attention to him because of his diminutive size, which was a mistake, since he tripped me up and made the tackle. I was embarrassed, to say the least.

When I was a junior, a new kid showed up at the beginning of the season. He was a good ballplayer, and he became the only starting sophomore on the team. We hit it off right away. His name is Terry Shields, and we played next to each other on the defensive line. Terry had been a state-champion wrestler in Arizona, and his claim to fame is that he pinned me twice, in twelve or thirteen seconds. He says it was twelve, and I say it was thirteen—so it was thirteen, since this is my book.

Terry Shields:

I remember when I first met Bill. Actually, I met his father first, because when I first reported to football practice, Dr. Goldberg gave me my physical. I couldn't play until I had a physical, and there wasn't a team doctor available, so I was given a checkup by an obstetrician/gynecologist.

My football coach was the attendance counselor, so we didn't get in trouble that much. We got away with about everything humanly possible. Terry and I would frequently bring the coach lunch on the way back from the doctor's office or wherever we said we were. If we didn't have a car to go out for lunch, the coach loaned us his. When we got into trouble with other teachers, they would send us to the coach. We used this time to go over football plays for the upcoming game.

When I started playing high school football, my life improved drastically. It was great—I was sixteen years old, making money, driving my dad's Jag, and dragging other cars through the streets of Clairemore, Oklahoma. I knew that I was getting out of town soon, and I was having fun. I didn't have many friends—Charlie Downs, Terry Shields, Adam Singer, and Bill Morris were my best friends. It's funny, I didn't have a lot of good friends at the time, but I have a lot now when I go back to Tulsa. Terry is still one of my best friends, and he takes care of my house in Georgia. With my crazy schedule, his help has been invaluable.

Me and Mom.

I didn't grow up watching my father wrestle, I grew up watching my brothers play football, so I've always looked at wrestling as a business. It was never a dream of mine, and if it had been, I might have approached it differently. My whole childhood was consumed with thoughts of playing football for a living and then retiring.

Booker T. Washington High was one of our cross-city rivals, and their star lineman was Eric Johnson. We played against each other since the eighth grade, and we became good friends. He helped make me a better player, and thus contributed to my success. Eric's a great guy, and I love him to death. We both wanted to play major college football, and as it turned out, we traveled down the path to pursue our dream together at college. This was a blessing because we watched each other's backs and helped each other adjust.

chapter twelve

GOIN' TO THE DAWGS

I was in the ninth grade when I received my first recruiting letter. William and Mary wanted me to become a member of the Tribe (which I already thought I was). This was the beginning of the next phase of fulfilling my ultimate football dream. By the beginning of my senior year, I was receiving a steady stream of recruiting letters in the mail and recruiters at my door. I was contacted by quite a number of major colleges, including two through my family connections. Both of my brothers had played football for the University of Minnesota, and my great-uncle played for the University of Georgia. My father played for Harvard and Johns Hopkins, but they weren't exactly football powerhouses. And I wasn't exactly their kind of student.

My mother's uncle, Louis Wolfson, had followed my high school career and he offered to contact his alma mater, the University of Georgia, on my behalf. Knowing their football tradition and emphasis on defense, I decided to take him up on his offer. Lou had lettered in football in 1931, and thanks to a hefty donation, the first floor of the Butts-Mehre football building at Georgia bears his name. He is better known for owning a racehorse by the name Affirmed, who happens to be the last horse to win the coveted Triple Crown.

Like my brothers, I wanted to go out of state for college. I wanted a fresh start, far away from the problems I'd endured growing up in Tulsa. Deep down I always thought that if you're truly a good player you could go where no one knew you and make a name for yourself. As for the University of Minnesota, I had been there enough visiting my brothers to know how miserably cold it gets in winter. Both Mike and Steve told me flat out to go elsewhere. When I notified U. of M. head coach Lou Holtz that I had decided to attend Georgia, he became indignant, and barked out in his nasal drawl, "Why would a Jewish boy like you want to play with *those* people in the Deep South?" I still wonder who *those* people were that he was referring to, because for me, there was no better place to play football than the South.

I went on recruiting trips to various places, including the Universities of Oklahoma, Texas, Miami, Arkansas, Missouri, and Georgia at Athens. Like most recruits, I had a great time on all of my visits, but from what I can remember, Georgia was the best. (Even better than my Missouri trip, when I was snowed in for four days with their aerobics instructor.) I had so much fun that I was surprised they followed through with their scholarship offer.

Not only was I being recruited by these schools, so were my parents.

Jed Goldberg:

The head coach of Arkansas, Kenneth Hatfield, wrote to me to assure me that they would take care of Bill's needs, both physical and spiritual. I accompanied Bill on the recruiting trip to Fayetteville, and when I toured the coaches' offices, there was a bible on every desk. Afterward, Bill received a call from one of the assistant coaches (I think his name was Goldman), and he told Bill that he would pay special attention to him because he, too, was Jewish. "Was" is the key word here, because I remember reading an article in the sports pages of the *Miami Herald* that recounted the story of how at the age of sixteen, Coach Goldman, or whoever he was, became a born-again Christian.

Another time, I accompanied Bill to the University of Texas, and I was driving back to the hotel in Austin with one of the assistant coaches. He looked at me, and in a very serious manner said, "Doctor, right this very moment, Coach Akers is offering a full scholarship to your son." It was like Bill was being awarded the Nobel Prize. And he went on to say, "The only condition is that he has to say yes to the offer at this very moment, because he only gets one chance." And I said, "Well, knowing my son Bill, he won't be going to Texas, because he's not the kind of person who will be hurried into a decision." And sure enough, that's what Bill told the head coach. Strangely enough, after we returned home, the calls from Texas kept coming. They said that they had to draw a line in the sand, but I guess the tide came in and washed it away.

Since my dad had accompanied me on my last trip, to the University of Arkansas, I felt compelled to play the give-equal-time-to-both-divorced-parents game, so my mom and I headed down to Dixie.

We arrived in Atlanta, and I was shuttled to Athens by helicopter, and my mother drove there with one of the assistant coaches. Mom and I split up for the evening, and we were scheduled to meet again the next morning, for breakfast with legendary head coach Vince Dooley. I was entertained by members of the football squad, whose sole purpose was to get me hammered. Although the memory is still a bit fuzzy, I think they deserved All-SEC honors for their effort. Meanwhile, my mother was being wined and dined by the coaches, who I'm sure had an entirely different agenda.

Steve Boswell, Scott Adams, and Larry Brown took me to one of the local football hangouts, the Jamestown apartment complex. I don't remember much, but I vaguely remember swaying shirtless on a table, swigging from a bottle of Wild Turkey and erupting like Mount Vesuvius.

Larry Brown and I celebrate our 1987 Liberty Bowl victory over Arkansas.

Larry Brown:

My first impression of Bill was: This boy could be a Bulldog.
He definitely could be a dawg, 'cause he ran hard. The way we
judged whether we wanted someone to come to Georgia or not
was if they really partied. We had this concept that if you were
a hard partyer, you were a hard player, and you're going to fit in
better. The wilder you were off the field, the wilder you were on
the field.

I slept through my wake-up call and hid under the covers until
my host, Steve Boswell, finally woke me up an hour after I was supposed to be at breakfast. What he found was not a pretty sight; in

fact, it was a pretty stinky sight. It was snowing outside and not much warmer in my room, because I had gone to sleep with the windows wide open. I had puked all over, and the way it smelled and the way I looked were pretty disgusting. I somehow threw myself together, and Boswell aimed me in the direction of my meeting with Coach Dooley. I found my mother seated next to the coach, and she took one look at me and proclaimed, "Oh, my god, it looks like Bill drank half of Georgia last night." Thanks, Mom.

Coach Ray Goff:

I think Bill had a rather large time in Athens. I don't think there's any doubt about it. On Saturday morning, after going out Friday night with some of the players, Bill's eyes looked like two pee holes in the snow.

I can remember when Bill told me that he was coming to Georgia. The weekend he was here on his official visit, he told me, personally; he said, "I'm coming to Georgia." Of course, the next weekend he was going to visit Oklahoma and Barry Switzer and all that Oklahoma faction. Oklahoma was pretty good at the time, and we were pretty good, too. I kept telling him, "Bill, they're gonna talk to you. Don't let them change your mind." He said, "Coach, I told you I'm coming to Georgia, and that's where I'm going!" He was true to his word.

Coach Vince Dooley:

At that particular time, Oklahoma University was in its prime, and to say no to Oklahoma and Barry Switzer, if you were in-state, you had to have a pretty extra incentive to want to leave, because they put on a good show and they recruited hard. There were very few that got out of the state during that era, so we figured we had a lot of things going for us. It was a major coup to get Bill out of Oklahoma.

I almost didn't go to UGA because of the legendary freshman initiation rite, known as Seagraves. Fortunately, it was discontinued the year before I started. It took place after the season, in the spring, and it was the coming of age, rite of acceptance onto the team. It took place in the middle of nowhere, at a resort called Poss's Lakeside, which was owned by Georgia alumnus Bobby Poss. The torture began with a trip to the Varsity Restaurant for hot dogs and Cook's beer. This ritual alone would kill a normal man. The freshmen were forced to eat large quantities of dogs and wash them down with fresh-off-the-fire, warm Cook's beer. Then they were stripped naked and made to stand back-to-back and hook each other by the arms. They would then alternate lifting each other up off the ground, as upperclassmen came around and punched the suspended freshman in the gut until he threw up MEAT. I'm no pussy, but I wouldn't have let myself be a part of that, because there's only so much shit I'll take to do what I want to do.

Seagraves was finally called off after one of the freshmen almost died during the initiation. He'd had enough abuse, and when he jumped one of the upperclassmen, another guy jumped in and cold-cocked the freshman. The poor guy ended up swallowing his tongue, almost choking to death.

Scott Adams:

At Seagraves, if a freshman wanted to call out an upperclassman, he could call him out and go brawl with him. That's what happened, one of the guys was messing with freshman Otis Jones, and they started fighting. Andy Loy wasn't going to stand there and watch a freshman fight one of his teammates, so after about a hundred-yard sprint, he forearmed poor Otis in the jaw, breaking it in three places. Otis swallowed his tongue, and me and Troy Sadowski were freshmen going through the initiation, and we had to go get a stick and pry his mouth open so

Coach Kasay could pull Otis's tongue out without having his fingers bit off. It was pretty insane.

When I started at Georgia, they assured me that they had discontinued freshman hazing, but they lied. Right after two-a-days ended in the fall, we were put through a modified version of Seagraves, called Rat Corps. One afternoon, all of the freshmen were assembled in the courtyard in front of the athletic dorm and told to strip down to our shorts. Then we had to form an elephant line, which is where you bend over and put one hand between your legs and grab the outstretched hand of the guy behind you. Then he does the same to the guy behind him, and so on and so on. We paraded around like this for a while, singing some strange chant that made absolutely no sense whatsoever. Then we had to go down the stairs of the athletic dorm with our eyes closed, and if we opened them, they sealed them shut with a deep-heating ointment, Icy Hot. For added measure, they'd seal our butt cracks with Icy Hot, too. All the time, they were pissing and spitting on us from the top levels of the dorm.

Then we had to get in front of the Grand Dragon, who was a 375-pound black guy named Keith Johnson, who, oddly enough, was dressed in an all-white KKK suit. We had to tell him how *bad* we were, and if what you said didn't entertain him, you had to go back to the end of the line.

For added enjoyment, they unloaded a whole truckful of warm, steaming cow shit, which they spread out so we could do some push-ups over it.

Scott Adams:

Throughout the year, the freshmen had to do stuff for the upperclassmen, like wash their car or run errands. In return, they had a big brother to look after them. Larry Brown was my

big brother, and I was Bill's. When I was a red-shirt freshman and
Bill was a freshman, they had already done away with Seagraves,
and that was the last year they had Rat Corps. Other schools
were using it against Georgia for recruiting. They said, "If you go
to Georgia, you're going to get the shit beat out of you." It was
really all about who wanted to be a player. Who wanted to make
the sacrifice.

I survived Rat Corps and settled into the college routine. As a
true freshman, I didn't suit up and I didn't travel with the team, so
game days were party days. One day, we were playing Auburn at
home, so we started our warm-ups at Jamestown apartments, which
was *the* place to party on campus. The team would stay in Madison,
Georgia, the night before home games, and Jamestown happened to
be on the way back to Sanford Stadium. It was a direct route, so we
knew when they were going to pass by there every game. The freshmen got on the roof of the apartment complex, and spelled out KICK
AUBURN'S ASS with paint on our butt cheeks. As the bus passed,
Coach Dooley looked at Larry Brown and Scott Adams, and said in
his deep Southern drawl, "Ahr those friends of yours?" He had no
idea that it was the whole freshman team . . . until now, that is!

The next year they really cracked down on Seagraves and Rat
Corps, and didn't let us do anything to the freshmen. After all of the
shit we took, we were finally in a position to dish some out . . . we
decided we'd earned the right. We were going to make damn sure
that, one way or another, the freshmen were going to suffer. In the
fall of my sophomore year, Scott Adams and I created our own little initiation.

All freshmen are required to run the mile-plus-mile endurance
test, where they run a mile under a certain time limit and then, after
only a three-minute rest, they have to do it again. The evening
before the big run, Scott and I assembled as many of those freshmen
guys as we could get ahold of, and lined them up in the front parking lot of McWhorter Hall. Scott and I were feeling kind of froggy

that day, so we put a keg of beer in the back of his truck and parked it on the steps of the dorm. We had all the freshmen line up in three-point stances, and we'd tee up golf balls and drive them across the parking lot for them to retrieve. Whoever got the ball first was the lucky one who could rest for a while.

After a few beers, Scott and I and a couple of other guys grabbed as many freshmen as we could and shaved their heads. We wanted to be creative so we shaved some like Hare Krishnas and gave others the horseshoe or the arrow cut. Some we shaved bald. Coach Dooley found out about our little ritual and he was quite pissed off, but it was worth it.

Every opportunity we had, we bucked the system. There were so many rules—they told you when to eat and sleep and take a dump. You were always in meetings, and everything you did had to do with football. Whether it was missing curfew or staying out all night on a drunk, it didn't matter . . . even if it was during two-a-days. We went all out and we were as wild as we possibly could be. And at that age, our bodies could take the abuse and bounce right back.

Larry Brown was from Dublin, Georgia, near Wrightsville, where Herschel Walker came from. It was two and a half hours from Athens, and right next to the O'Hoopie swamp. That's where Larry and his friends taught me how to be a redneck. Here I was, this Jewish boy from Oklahoma who was bar mitzvahed in a synagogue five years before, and I was in the O'Hoopie swamp washing dishes with mossy green water and wiping my ass with huckleberries.

Scott Adams:

Everywhere you went was by dirt road and we went to a liquor store, and I heard the guy behind the counter tell a guy, "You could either buy the beer with cash or you could trade a couple of chickens in." For beer! Lake City is country, but nothing like this. This was like *Dukes of Hazzard* shit. You could buy beer with farm animals.

Once, we went on a road trip to Scott's home in Florida. His parents had a cabin at Ocean Pond, outside of his hometown, Lake City, and we went down there to party and hang out. John Brantley and I were sitting on a dock, and between the two of us, we downed a case of beer through a beer funnel. One of our friends, Bruce Fike, came by the dock in Scott's dad's boat, pulling a big inner tube behind it. I jumped in the water and got on the inner tube, then Brantley jumped in and grabbed ahold of me. When the boat took off, Brantley was thrown from the tube, and I went tumbling. I caught the rope with my hand and it wrapped around my arm. They were dragging me around the lake and I was yelling "whoooooa," and Fike thought I was saying "gooooooooo," so they kept going until we were halfway across the lake. When they finally stopped, I rose out of the water with nothing on but my jock strap, and my damn fingers were pulled halfway out of their sockets. There was a blood blister the size of Mount Rushmore on my hand, and it was so swollen that it looked like one of those big, goofy "number one" foam-rubber hands you see fans wear at football games.

Everyone thought I was really hurt, and decided that I should go to the hospital. I said, "Hell, I'll drive," and considering everyone else's condition, it seemed like a good idea. We went about twenty miles back to Lake City, which we made in about ten minutes. Scott's grandfather was a doctor in town, and since it was lunchtime when we got back, Scott knew that we could find him at the Moose Lodge. Scott went in to find him, and when he walked outside and took one look at me, he said, "You boys need to go to the emergency room." So we drove to the hospital, we checked in, and I gave the nurse my I.D. After sitting in the waiting room for about an hour and not being called, we noticed they kept calling the name Steve Smith. Finally I said, "Where is this guy?" and I realized that this was the name on my fake I.D., which I'd apparently given to her by mistake. We ended up just leaving, because we had waited so long that the blood blister went down on its own. We got in the car and drove back to the lake and resumed partying.

The crazy times I spent with Scott and Larry were some of the funniest experiences of my entire life. Like the time we closed up the Odyssey Bar and decided to go fishing in the middle of the night. We went to the store to get bait, and we ended up with baloney and hot dogs. Then we drove out to the middle of nowhere, until we ended up under a bridge on the river. The guys were fishing, and I was sitting on top of the cooler, and I was so messed up that when the guys weren't looking, I ate all of the bait. Scott said, "Give me some hot dogs," and I said, "I can't, I ate them all," so he said, "Give me some baloney, then," and I said, "I ate it all, too."

Out of disgust, Scott put on an artificial lure, and he cast his line into the darkened river. Out of nowhere he got a hit, and the line started going out—and his fish started flying away. He caught a damn duck! The duck was flying off with the lure, and Scott, being a responsible fisherman who believes in the catch-and-release philosophy, didn't set the hook. The duck got away.

There were fringe benefits from playing football, and I can't say that I didn't receive at least one favor from the faculty. A teacher who is no longer associated with the university, who will remain nameless, gave me a more than satisfactory grade for his class. I was astounded and pleased, considering my lack of attendance during the semester. My only interest in college was to use it as a stepping stone to the NFL—and of course, I loved the Georgia peaches. I always assumed that I knew enough to survive and get by because of the experiences that I had growing up with my family. I thought I was worldly beyond my years and that what I learned in school was a waste of time because it wouldn't help me on the football field . . . obviously I was wrong. Psychology was the only subject that interested me, and that's what I chose for my major.

There is another kind of preferential treatment you hear about, and it relates to the cushy jobs that you get when you play football. You see it in movies, and for the most part, it's true. About four or five days after I moved to Athens the summer before my freshman year, Eric Johnson and I were given jobs at a local auto dealership.

Eric was an archrival from high school but became my roommate at UGA. Our duties entailed showing up at about ten-thirty in the morning and leaving about one o'clock, after we had lunch with a few of the managers. Ironically, we were clocked in from nine to five. Go figure.

This job was especially cool for me, because I always wanted a Ford Mustang 5.0 and I was given a demo to try out for a while. The first day I had it, I was driving home, and while I was adjusting one of the T-tops, it grew wings and shattered into a million pieces on the pavement behind me. This was the beginning of my bad luck at the University of Georgia. A couple of days later, I got a D.U.I. in that car. Less than a week into my freshman year, I realized that I had started off on the wrong foot.

I was so lazy and lackadaisical that many times I'd wake up late and have to drive my car just to make it to class. I thought that it was better to pay a parking fine than to miss school, and by my senior year, the number of tickets I collected was probably equal to the number of days I went to class. When the authorities finally caught up with me, I ended up paying for almost every one of them. Not only did I have the record for the most tackles by an interior lineman at Georgia, I also had the record for the most parking tickets.

Larry Brown and I played next to each other on the defensive line, and boy, did we beat the shit out of people. We were a formidable pair.

Steve Greer (Defensive Line Coach):

We had some good linemen at Georgia, but Bill was special. He had a KNOCKOUT PUNCH! He would come across an offensive lineman with a forearm shiver that was really effective.

Vince Dooley:

Opponents respected Bill. You'd watch films and you'd see him pursuing the football, around the football, making plays. When he hit you, he hit you good. So, he got the coach's attention when they were getting ready to play us.

Billy Brewer (Former Ole Miss Coach):

Goldberg is a warlord, a knife-toting, gun-toting bad guy.

During a game against the University of Kentucky, an offensive lineman was blocking Larry after the play, and as I threw another offensive lineman off of me, I heard this *pop*. I turned around, and the guy that was messing with Larry was standing there just looking at him, and the guy's helmet was about ten feet up in the air. Larry had forearmed this guy's helmet right off his head, straight into the air.

The action didn't always stop at the end of the game when we played Kentucky. In 1988, they upset us 16–10, and dashed our hopes to play in the Sugar Bowl. I was one of the last guys off the field, and there was a fence that separated us from the fans. As I was walking off, real dejected, I saw my dad and my brother Mike standing at the fence. I walked over and started talking to them, and the fans were yelling at me and the other players over Mike and Jed's back. Mike got pissed off and it got to the point where he said, "Leave the kids alone." Someone said something else, and the next thing you know Mike turned around and shoved his portable TV down the guy's throat. All hell broke loose, and Mike and Jed ended up in the middle of the angry crowd. I scaled the fence and started throwing people out of the way so I could get to the middle and help my father.

Mike Goldberg:

I could take the taunting from the crowd until someone started yelling racial slurs. I told the guy to stop, and when he told me to fuck off, I cranked him.

As for my toughest opposition in college, I'd have to give Eric Andolcek top honors. Another standout far and away above the rest was Dermontti Dawson from Kentucky, who turned out to be an All-Pro for the Pittsburgh Steelers. Eric, god rest his soul, played for LSU, and after a shortened NFL career he was killed in a freak accident, when an eighteen-wheeler went out of control and hit him while he was mowing his front yard.

BILL GOLDBERG
Defensive Tackle/Nose Guard · #95
 6′3″ · 266
Tulsa, OK

1988 — All-American candidate entering 1988 season after 107-tackle performance in 1987, the most tackles by any Bulldog interior defensive lineman on record ... started every game at middle guard for the Bulldogs in '88 ... named to All-SEC team by United Press International and the SEC Coaches ... Major: Psychology.

Tips from the BULLDOGS
One way for the defense to stop an offensive drive is with a ferocious sack. Don't let people sack your drive for success with cocaine or crack. If you do, even the first time could stop your heart.

Special thanks to
The Charter Winds Hospital
Produced by: Bensussen-Deutsch
& Assoc., Inc., Redmond, WA

 CHARTER WINDS HOSPITAL

The first game I ever started I had to play against Eric, when the guy in front of me went down from an injury. I was a sophomore, and it was my first game, so you can probably guess the way I played. I was a human pinball. The next day as we were watching game films I made a startling discovery. On a certain play, the running back sped around the end of the line. I broke through the line and tried to run him down. A huge cleat hit me right in the ass. It was Andolcek. You got to love his tenacity. I was very respectful because he did what he had to do to get the job done. That was my total motivation for the next year. I prepared for him, all right; the next time we met on the football field, I made 21 tackles and recovered 2 fumbles.

One other instance that really sticks out in my mind about Eric occurred in the last game we faced each other. During that game we got an interception, and Larry and I were running right down the sideline, preparing to throw a block. I spotted Andolcek out of the corner of my eye. He was coming at us at an angle. Larry was behind me, and we both saw him, and since I was in front, Larry decided to give me a little push as his contribution. That sent me out of control, and as I went to hit Eric, he turned around, planted his foot, and hit me under my chin with his forearm. He saw me coming, and to say that he hit me with force would be an understatement. I did a back flip, and the first thing that hit the ground was my face mask. Larry saw the whole thing, and laughed uncontrollably, probably for the rest of the game. He'll never let me live that down.

We had a big rivalry with the University of Florida, and every year the game was played in the Gator Bowl in Jacksonville. This location was about the midpoint between the two schools, and the game was billed as the world's largest outdoor cocktail party, but playing the Gators was anything but a picnic. We always had great games against Florida, and one year I almost passed out before the game, I was so pumped up. We held Emmitt Smith to 32 yards when they were ranked number one in the nation. He was a great ballplayer, but I could see tears in his eyes as we were pounding him play after play after play.

When I was at Georgia, I was always thinking about where I was going to play football after college, and I was on track to fulfill my dream until the end of my junior year. We were going to play Michigan State in the Gator Bowl, and I would be lined up against their star offensive lineman, Tony Mandarich. Kicking his ass would give me great national exposure, not to mention great pleasure.

I was at a party with a bunch of my teammates, celebrating our berth in the bowl game. Unfortunately, it turned out I had nothing to celebrate. I failed my drug test. I don't know what you've heard or what's been proven about secondary smoke, but I'm here to tell you—that wasn't my alibi.

I was seriously bummed out, and I wasn't even allowed on the sidelines for the game. I decided to split and go to Miami and watch the game with my brother Mike. He had a fourteen-foot TV screen, which unfortunately made it even more painful to watch. Not only did it show that I messed up in a big way, it also showed what a jerk Joe Theisman really is. He was one of the commentators, and he went on and on about how I had let the team down and what a self-ish thing I had done. Well, Joe, you'll always be a pussy-ass quarterback to me, and you failed to mention that I was All-SEC and I was the all-time leader in tackles for a lineman at Georgia and I was ninth in sacks and an All-American and was one of the reasons we were in the damn game in the first place. You changed the pronunciation of your name to rhyme with "Heisman," for god's sake. By the way, Joe, blow me. Is it sadistic for me to wish that I was Lawrence Taylor, breaking Theisman's leg over and over again?

Granted, I did screw up really badly—I did let the team down in my decision to do what I did. I was a junior in college, and I still had one more year of eligibility. I had a very clean record up to then, and I would cut my right and left arms off for the team. Everybody knew that, not only on the team, but around the media and everywhere else. I do admit that what I did was wrong, but the way that he went about chastising me personally, that was definitely uncalled for.

At the beginning of my senior year, I was projected to be one of the top fifty picks in the country for the upcoming NFL draft. Unfortunately, by the end of the year I was closer to the bottom fifty. As the year evolved, the coaches changed my position from defensive tackle to defensive end, and I sustained more and more injuries.

Coach Ray Goff:

He had a lot of respect from the coaches because of the kind of player he was. He was hurt a lot. He had a lot of shoulder problems and neck problems, pinched nerves. He'd come out for a play or two, and then he'd go back in. As tough as he was, he'd bite nails and do anything to get back in the game. He really had a lot of pain his last year at Georgia, with the neck burners [pinched nerves] that he had. You couldn't help but admire him from that standpoint, because you knew the guy was giving it everything he had.

Coach Steve Greer:

Bill had skills and he knew the game. Mentally, they didn't come any tougher! He had the strength and the power, but I've never coached a kid as mentally tough as Bill Goldberg. Half the time he'd play one-handed. He'd hurt his shoulder and have to come out of the game, and you knew he was in pain, but before you knew it, he'd be wanting to get back in the game. You'd wonder how he could play all banged up like that, and he'd just say, "Coach, it's only one shoulder. I'm gonna play with the other one." And he'd go out there and do it.

By the end of the year I was a mere shadow of myself. In the third to the last game of the season, we played Florida, and I suffered a severe ankle injury. I could barely walk after the game, and I was on crutches the rest of the week. I got shot up so I could play the next game, at Auburn against All-American Ed King.

I got my ass handed to me, and the same thing happened to me the next week at Georgia Tech. The fact is, our team wasn't that good, and I didn't have a very good year. Combined with what happened at the end of my junior year, my pro outlook was bleak.

Georgia buddies—Blake Mitchel, Scott Adams, Craig Martin, Larry Brown, and Mack Burroughs.

Coach Ray Goff:

His senior year, we were not a great football team. We were 6–5 and I think we lost four games by a total of eleven points. I mean, we were in every game, and I think it was just because of him and the defense. We didn't have a lot of talent. We had a lot of guys who—they'd just cut their hearts out for you, and I think Bill was kind of the "lead pirate," so to speak.

BILL WOULD HAVE BEEN A GREAT COWBOY! He probably was born 150 years too late. Bill should have played college football in the '30s, '40s, '50s. He's just a throwback to the old days. You just don't find a lot of guys like Bill anymore. He played through pain. He's just a tough hombre.

Growing up in Oklahoma, all I really watched was Big Eight football. I didn't know much about other conferences. Of course, Georgia was in the SEC, and when I checked out the conference, I discovered that they were known pretty much for their defensive style of play. It wasn't a wide-open conference by any stretch of the imagination. They played a hunker-down style of football. The SEC was then and is now—and I think always will be—one of the toughest conferences. This is because there are so many teams that are equal in talent within the league. They beat the shit out of each other weekly, and by the end of the season, when they have to play postseason games and represent the conference, they're beaten up from playing interconference games.

When I got to Georgia, what stands out in my mind the most was our plethora of running backs. Herschel Walker graduated a number of years before I arrived. Cleveland Gary and Lars Tate were a couple of years ahead of me, and in my class we had Tim Worley and Keith Henderson. A couple of years after them, we had Rodney Hampton and Garrison Hearst; and a couple of years after them, we had Terrell Davis. Our stable of running backs were so good that Cleveland Gary left when Tim Worley and Keith Henderson came in as freshmen. He transferred to the University of Miami. Even though Terrell Davis didn't play much at Georgia, he went on to play for the Broncos, and ultimately became a Super Bowl MVP.

It was an extremely tough conference. It was smash-mouth, beat-'em-up football. There wasn't a lot of passing going on. It was ground 'em and pound 'em . . . just like this wrestling style I'm employing right now.

University of Georgia Honors

All-SEC Associated Press first team: junior year, 1988; senior year, 1989

All-American second team, *Football News:* 1989 (behind Moe Gardner, Chris Zorich, and Tim Ryan; Russell Maryland was third team)

All-American, Mizlou Network: senior year (oh, boy!)

All-time tackles: ninth (348)

Primary tackles: eighth (170)

Parking tickets: 150, yearly average

Tackle assists: sixth (178)

Quickest D.U.I.: 5th day on campus

Quarterback sacks: ninth (12)

Most single season tackles for a lineman (121)

Most alcohol consumed by a recruit

J. B. Whitworth Award (outstanding lineman, UGA, 1989)

I kept this note on my door at college.

W. CARL LINDSTROM, M.D.
DEA NO. AL2132138

HALL KETCHUM, M.D.
DEA NO. AK2132152

JED E. GOLDBERG, M.D.
DEA NO. AG2132140

DAVID K. HAGGARD, M.D.
DEA NO. AH 2132164

JOHN M. SHANE, M.D.
DEA NO. AS7734418

OBSTETRICS AND GYNECOLOGY
REPRODUCTIVE ENDOCRINOLOGY AND INFERTILITY
Suite 304, Warren Professional Building

6465 South Yale Avenue

Tulsa, Oklahoma 74136

Phone 492-5511

NAME _____

DATE _____

ADDRESS _____

℞

Dear Son,

There's an old saying in Latin "carborundum non illegitimatum" which loosely translates as "don't let the bastards wear you down"

Love Dad,

LABEL CONTENTS

Rept. ut dictum
2 3 4 times
PRN ☐ Non Rept. ☐

Tulsa, Oklahoma _____, M.D.

chapter thirteen

PROS AND CONS

Ram It!

The season ended, and I was hoping to redeem myself after my miserable senior year and the Gator Bowl fiasco. Though we went to a postseason bowl game—the Peach Bowl in Atlanta—nothing more should be said. The only other opportunity I had to prove myself to pro scouts came when I was selected to play in the Japan Bowl. As my luck would have it, I caught mono two weeks before the game, and I lost about twenty pounds. I was down to 245 pounds at game time, and I was weak from being sick. I think the combination of events greatly reduced the value of my stock, as evidenced by the fact that I wasn't invited to the NFL combines. Not that it would have helped too much.

By draft day, I was pretty dejected. There I sat for a day and a half at my brother Mike's house in Miami, wondering if I was going to be selected at all. Finally the phone call came, and I was headed to L.A. I was taken in the eleventh round by the Rams. My dream was still alive.

When I arrived in camp, I felt like shit, because I was one of the top fifty guys at the beginning of my senior year and I had to wait until the second day of the draft to be taken by the Rams. I felt like I had a hell of a lot to prove and they weren't giving me any respect . . . maybe I didn't deserve any. I was prepared mentally and physically, but I knew that I had a lot to overcome.

The first day in camp, I walked into the weight room, and to my amazement one of the linemen was doing biceps curls with 305 pounds. I said to myself, "Am I in the right fricking place?" Ironically, weeks later, during the NFL drug test, that same person came out of the bathroom stirring his piss, go figure.

Our offensive line consisted of Tom Newberry, Jackie Slater, Joe Milinichik, Duval Love, Irv Pankey, and Doug Smith, and they were enormous. One player was prone to holding out, and you knew when he was in camp, because there would be a big, used Tucks hemorrhoids pad stuck to the clock in the training room. This gesture signified his return. Needless to say, I've dealt with some pretty gross people throughout my athletic career.

Every practice was nerve-racking, because I was on trial and I always had something to prove. Every day I thought I was going to get cut, and I thought of my brother Steve and the times that he was axed from pro teams. This time I didn't want to follow in his footsteps, and hiding under my bed was not my style.

Draft Day—the call finally came from the Rams.

I did fairly well from practice to practice, but it was hard to gain confidence without encouragement from the coaches. Finally, the defensive coordinator, Fritz Shurmer, began to notice me and comment on my play. That helped a lot, and my confidence started to build as I found that I had no problem competing on the professional level. The more I played, the better I felt about my chances of making the team, and by the next to last preseason game, I was feeling pretty damn good.

We were going to play the Kansas City Chiefs in the American Bowl, which, oddly enough, was being played in Berlin. We arrived five days before the game, and we had joint practices with the Chiefs. They were held at Olympic Stadium, which was where Hitler used to give ranting speeches to his troops. I felt quite uneasy being in a country where my ancestors were killed. This feeling prompted me to take the "Goldberg" off the back of my jersey. I was very uneasy there, and I envisioned myself hiding behind trees, trying to get away.

After practice and meetings, I hung out with teammates Frank Stamms and Paul Butcher, and Danny Salamua from the Chiefs. Two nights before the game, we all went out and consumed a great deal of warm German beer and put a dent in the local bratwurst population. We stayed out all night, and when I finally stumbled to my room, my roommate, Burn Brostic, wouldn't let me in. Time was of the essence, I was about to explode. Unfortunately, disaster struck shortly thereafter. I think the smell was so bad that Burn finally opened the door out of pity. I won't go into details, but let's just say that I got in the shower fully clothed. I don't really know what happened, but somehow I made it to my bed and the next thing I knew I was awakened from my haze by loud knocking at the door. It was Frank and Paul. I said, "Hey man, you guys ready to go to practice?" "Practice?" Frank said. "We're ready to go to dinner." I said, "What are you talking about?" and Paul explained, "You *slept* through practice!"

I had slept through the entire practice! Anyway, the coaches had asked about me but when they sent somebody up to check on me, nobody answered the door. He did notice a foul odor emanating from my room, so the coaches sent a doctor up to see me. I conned him into believing that I had food poisoning. The room smelled so bad that I think he just agreed so he could get the hell out of there. He gave me a couple of shots, and Frank and Paul were sitting in the corner laughing at me, and I was hard-pressed not to crack up. After missing practice, being fined was the least of my worries. I thought I'd be cut and sent home immediately. At that point, I would have paid to stay there, but much to my surprise, I never got fined or sent home. I was scared shitless, because I was a rookie and my dream was in jeopardy.

So, the next day, I came out with fire shooting through my nostrils. We went right into one-on-one pass rush drills with the Chiefs. Much to my surprise, I was lined up against one of my all-time heroes, Mike Webster. Though I revered him for being the dominating center for the Pittsburgh Steelers, the Mike Webster in front of me today was a mere shadow of himself. Not only was he about 220 years old, he was only 220 pounds. I put my feelings of reverence aside, and Mike Webster soon became the recipient of my urgent quest to redeem myself. I had to kill people, and even though it was his last year, I didn't care who I was lined up against. I tried to fight everybody on their team—Will Shields, Frank Zott, Tim Grunyard. I remember fighting every one of them and enjoying it. I had to show what I could do. I came back to the States feeling even better about my chances of making the team.

I had only one preseason game to go, and if I had a good game, I was on the squad. We were playing St. Louis. Things were going great . . . until the last kickoff of the game. On the prior kickoff, I ran down the field all pumped up, and hit special teams veteran Craig Wolfly, knocking him into the end zone. He got up laughing at me! You gotta respect that! But the next time down I wanted to kill him. In my haste to run down and finish the job, I forgot to stretch. When I got about halfway down the field, it felt like I was shot by a sniper. I had torn my hamstring.

Of course, I was worried about my status after the game, but as I was hobbling away from the stadium on crutches, dejected, one of my coaches approached me. He told me not to worry, because I had played well and my chances of making the team were good. That was the first time I was lied to in the NFL, and it wasn't the last.

Pro football lesson number one: Never trust a football coach.

The next day, Coach Robinson called me into his office and released me, and they gave me a few bucks for my injury and told me to hit the road.

I usually didn't allow myself to feel compassion for the other guys vying for my position, but I did become friends with a very good guy by the name of Anthony Bruno. He was just like me—fighting futilely to pursue his dream. But also like me, he was released. To this day, we're still good friends.

I didn't have many alternatives at the time, so I moved to Miami and worked for Mike and rehabbed. Once my leg healed, it was too late to catch on with another team, and I had to wait until the next season.

Since the Rams had liked me so much my rookie season (yeah, right!), I was excited to hear that they wanted me back the next year. Fritz Shurmer really liked me, so I thought that I had an advantage playing for him. Fritz was a great guy, but that didn't do me any good, because he and the rest of the coaching staff were released shortly after I re-signed with the team. They were replaced by Chuck Knox, and his defensive coordinator was Jeff Fisher. I sensed right away that I didn't have a prayer with the new coaching staff. They knew little about me, and I was basically ignored during practice. It was very, very discouraging having to stand around, watching from the sidelines, knowing that they could give a rat's ass about me.

There were a few people who influenced my life during that time. Jackie Slater had been in the league for a long time, maybe fifteen years, and I very much respected him. He was All-Pro and a legend, and to me he was what the old-style football player was all about. I listened to everything he said, and watched what he did. He was a big influence on me.

And so was Jack Youngblood. He was through playing for the Rams, but he was a coach, and he was in the weight room every damn day. He was the only person who was in there as much as I was. He was a hard-nosed, rough-ass defensive end, and he was everything that I admired when I was a kid. He was a tough country boy who loved to play football, and that was what it was all about. He went out and played in the Super Bowl with a broken leg . . . so, what was not to like about him?

Garrett Giemont was the weight coach, and it seems that I became a good friend with the weight coach on every team I played with. Go figure. Garrett showed me the ropes, and he helped me build confidence. I learned a lot from him. And I want to mention Todd, the equipment manager, because he was a good guy, and if the equipment manager didn't like you, he didn't wash your stuff.

Another person that stood out with the Rams was Bill Hawkins. Bill played college ball at the University of Miami, which was a breeding ground for unusual characters. One day we were sitting in a defensive-line meeting when he received a package. He opened it, and to his surprise, it was his sister's placenta on dry ice. We were all stunned. He always joked with her that when she had a baby, he wanted the placenta, and boy, did she give it to him. He in turn gave it to the equipment manager, who buried it behind a tree. The final chapter was during practice when his dog dug it up and ate it. Yum, yum!

Then there were Kevin Green and Paul Butcher. Kevin was another SEC guy, who played at Auburn. His passion for playing football was unrivaled. He retired the all-time sack leader for outside linebackers. Boy, was he a nut. But his help was invaluable during my rough times with the Rams. During my last stint with the Rams, we were roommates, which turned out to be a great deal. When you're of Kevin's stature, you tend to get perks. During training camp, our defensive-line coach would come by and bring him cold beers, which he fortunately shared. Butcher was a stocky linebacker from Wayne State, located somewhere in Detroit. He was one bad hombre. His tenacity earned him a spot on the All-Madden team one year. He had played with a number of other teams and gave me a lot of encouragement.

When I was with the Rams the second time, it was extremely depressing, because I knew from the beginning that I didn't have a snowball's chance in hell of making the team. My brother Steve used to drive up from San Diego and watch practice, and we would go out for sushi afterward. I don't know what I would have done without his support, because I was watching my dream fly out the window. When we would have to go back to the training camp after dinner, it was like he was driving me to my execution. The ax was going to fall, but I didn't know when. I still have the letters that he wrote trying to cheer me up, and he spoke from experience, having been down that road before.

I was about as low as anytime in my life. I was a salmon swimming upstream against a tsunami, and the only place I was headed was somebody's sushi plate. Midway through the preseason, I was in the middle of practice when someone pulled me out of the defensive huddle and told me to report to the office. There I sat, in full pads in front of an administrative guy named Bill Shaw, and he cut me on the spot.

Surge . . . Not the Cola

After the Rams released me the second time, there was no interest at all from other teams. It was mid preseason, and there was a glut of more experienced players on the market, and I was a two-time loser with the same team. There was no way to explain that I had virtually made the team the first year and I didn't have a chance the second. I was just a profile, a number—and with the NFL my number was less than zero.

In fact, I was so low that I seriously considered playing in the Canadian Football League. The British Columbia Lions were interested in me, and they sent me a plane ticket to come up and meet with them. When I boarded that plane and headed to the great Northwest, most of my baggage wasn't in my suitcase. I had a lot of trepidation boarding that flight, because Canadian football was definitely a step down from the NFL; I had no idea how far down until I arrived at the team facility. It was like I had stepped on the football elevator and ended up back on the first floor of Edison High.

When I arrived in Vancouver, I went to the hotel, checked in, and went out for some dinner. When I returned to my room, I discovered that the dormant nightclub below had come to life, and the room was shaking to the disco beat. I called the front desk and requested a room change, and they moved me to the only available room in the hotel, which turned out to be located above the other end of the bar, directly above the other set of speakers. The only difference was that this new room had a little better bass and I got to hear the music from the other channel.

After a restless night, I pondered the situation and assessed my options. The team offered me a contract that would place me on the practice squad, for five hundred dollars a week—and I think that was Canadian. In addition, they wanted me to lose thirty pounds so I could adjust to their style of football. The defensive players had to line up three yards off the line of scrimmage, and almost every down was a pass play. This did not look like a very good vehicle to take me back to the NFL, but I didn't have any better option at the time. I was going to meet with the head coach after practice, so I arrived in time to tour their facility and catch a little of their workout. I watched for a while and talked to a few of the players, then I proceeded to check out their weight room. When I walked through the door, it was surreal, like a bad dream. The weight room at my high school was bigger, and better equipped. I was scheduled to leave after I met with the coaches, but I turned around and walked out that door and kept on going. I booked an earlier flight and high-tailed it back to the States.

While I was up in Vancouver, I received a glimmer of hope in the form of a look-see with the Miami Dolphins. They contacted my agent, and I flew down to Miami for a tryout. My dejection had a temporary reprieve, but it was evident that their interest was minimal. I went to their training facility, and I was put through a short workout of running and agility drills. Then I talked with head coach Don Shula on the sidelines, and he mostly talked to me about my brother Mike, who he knew from around Miami. Then he said, "So long," and that basically was it. He should have added "sucker" at the end, because I sure felt like one.

Unfortunately, I wasn't making it in the NFL, and there was another route that I had to take. The World Football League was an option, and although it wasn't one that I chose, it was one that I settled for as another pathway back to the NFL. In the second year of the World Football League, the Sacramento Surge made me their seventh-round selection.

Kay Stephenson:

We were high on Bill. We had seen tape from UGA. Everything we heard was good. Initial quickness, consistent hustler, motor was always running, relentless, always in the middle of the action.

The days playing for Sacramento were very good times. It was
the most fun football experience of my life. We were professionals
getting paid to do a job, yet the atmosphere was very lackadaisical.
It brought together a lot of good guys, from a lot of different places,
for one goal—to play football and have fun and try to make it to
the next level. There were older guys who had lost a step, and young
guys who never really got a shot at the NFL. Many of them were
never drafted because they were from small schools. It was a combination of people from everywhere. If we made it to the NFL, then
that was great, but either way, we had the experience to hold on to.

Jim Haslett (Defensive Coordinator):

**These were guys who were out of football and wanted to
play again,** or guys who were allocated to us from other teams.
There were guys who were out in the street. Guys who wanted
second shots, like Bill. Renegades, good guys, bad guys. There
was a little of everything there. Just guys who we tried to form
into a team.

The coaches weren't as strict as they were in the NFL, nor were
the rules of the team, but the level of play was very competitive. A
step down, for sure, but it was a hell of a lot of fun. It was football
again, and it was a lot less stressful, because it was more of a game
and less of a business.

Jim Haslett (On the WFL Experience):

We took a trip one time and went from Sacramento to San
Francisco, San Francisco to Dallas, Dallas to Birmingham, played
a game. We lost! Then we bussed to Atlanta. Stayed there three
days. Left from Atlanta to Detroit, Detroit to New York City, New
York City to London. We played a game and won! Went from
London to New York, New York to Montreal, and actually played a
game and won. Went from Montreal to New York, New York to

Dallas, Dallas to San Francisco. And bussed home. We played
Frankfurt, and won that game. When you got off the plane you
didn't know what your record was or where you were going, but
I just remember we had fun together.

The league was like *North Dallas Forty,* it was full of characters.
It so happened that a lot of the characters were on my team. There
was one guy who was famous for his affinity for golden showers.
Eric Neese, our punter, was a Calvin Klein model and one of the
original characters on *The Real World* on MTV. Pete Najerian played
linebacker for Tampa Bay for a number of years, and his father is a
world-famous heart transplant surgeon. Michael Sinclair was a
defensive end allocated from Seattle, who just so happens to be an
NFL All-Pro right now. On the other end was George Bethune from
the Rams. And then there was our tight end, Paul Greene, A.K.A.
Superman, whose nickname was derived from the fact that he was
supernaturally endowed for a white boy.

We had some established players, like our quarterback, David
Archer, who played with the Falcons, and running back Mike
Pringle, who played with Baltimore. We had some great players. Kay
Stephenson, the old Bills coach, was our head coach, and Jim
Haslett was the defensive coordinator. Jim used to be a formidable
ballplayer, and now he's the head coach of the New Orleans Saints.
We had a bunch of guys' guys. Jack Youngblood was one of our
defensive-line coaches, and he was one of the coolest guys and one
of my idols. The fact he was one of my coaches exemplifies how cool
my experience in the World League was. The atmosphere was laid-
back but competitive, and fortunately we were very good. We made
it all the way through the playoffs, and we won the World Bowl.

Jim Haslett (On the WFL Championship Game):

We were in Montreal the night before we played the championship game against Orlando. I decided I was going to do bed-check to make sure that everybody was in, and to see what was going on. I opened up Bill's room, and he's got some girl in bed, and I just looked at him and said, "You better play your ass off tomorrow!" I shut the door, went back down to the head coach. "Everything all right?" Coach Stephenson asked. I said, "Yep. Everybody's in bed, tucked in!" And Bill played a great game! He went out and had a heck of a game!

I made thirty-five thousand dollars, and it showed that we would do almost anything to be able to play pro football. So, right then I was like a professional wrestler doing the independents. It was good playing for the Surge, because my family could come up and watch me play, and it was like college again, except we got paid. And best of all, it propelled me back up to the NFL.

Jim Haslett:

We were in Montreal after winning the World Bowl, and we all went out. I'm sure some of the players went back to the strip joint. Most of us sat around, celebrated, and drank. We had a good time. It was a weird feeling, because we were coming back on the plane the next day, and guys were passing helmets and jerseys, and everybody knew on that plane that the forty-two guys we had were probably never going to see each other or be together again. It was a weird feeling.

Kay Stephenson:

Bill would have played for years and been a superstar in the NFL had he been bigger. He didn't have the bulk, didn't have great size, and that hurt him.

Bill played the game of football the way you're supposed to. I've coached good football players, many I respect, but none more than Bill Goldberg. He was the ideal guy to have on our football team. He's a throwback to the '40s and '50s. He had a relentless work ethic. In tight games, he was the heart and soul of our team. He'd keep everybody on their toes. He'd make key tackles, and always played with a never-say-die attitude, and he demanded that others follow suit. His enthusiasm was contagious, and that was important. He helped others make big plays simply because of his attitude. If we could have had twenty-two Bill Goldbergs on our football team, we would have been unbeatable!

Falcons

Three weeks after the World Bowl, I reported to the Falcons for preseason camp. I was in great shape, but I was pretty beat up after playing a complete season, the playoffs, and the World Bowl with the Surge. I had had just about enough football for that spring, but the opportunity to get back to the NFL was what I had worked so hard for, and I didn't care if it was three days or three weeks, I was excited. I knew I was in for a hard time, because every night Eric Peagram wanted me to sneak out and go drinking with him. After just having completed an entire season with the Surge, how could I say no? Hell, I was from the University of Georgia—I knew a lot of people, and I was playing for the hometown team.

I knew that I could compete at the pro level, but I had to try that much harder. I had to look for tricks, because I didn't have the overall athletic ability and size that a lot of guys had. I had to work harder in the gym. I had to be meaner and more determined than the rest, and I had to find an advantage. I had always been pretty strong . . . at least I thought I was until I started working out with the guys from the Falcons.

Tim Green (Defensive End):

Bill was the type of guy who was there because he worked his ass off. You might have been faster than him. You might have been quicker. You might have had more size, more strength, but you better bring your lunch pail if you're going up against Bill, because he got to where he was—and I think he got to where he is—because of his tenacity and his unwillingness to be out-worked.

I knew I was outclassed, outmanned, and unprepared when I met Jumpy Gathers. He was one of the guys that I was playing behind, and he was six foot seven and 320 pounds. One day during camp, Jessie Tuggle and I were doing presses with 150-pound dumbbells. Jumpy walked into the weight room with a lit cigar in his mouth, picked up one of the dumbbells, and just started pressing it like it was nothing . . . just puffing on that stogie. It was frustrating, to say the least.

Another time, I'd been working out on the neck machine, and I had two forty-five-pound weights on the rack. I thought my neck was strong, until Mike Richter walked over and put *four* forty-five-pound plates on the machine for his workout. He was using twice the weight I was; I just shook my head in amazement.

I needed an advantage, and I picked it up the first day of practice, when I figured out that I could read the lips of the quarterback in the huddle. I knew the snap count, so I had an added edge getting off the line. I swear to god, I made so many tackles that way that it isn't even funny . . . or maybe it is. I learned how to use my head at an early age, and not just for pounding it against walls.

I made a good impression, and I fought hard to make the team, and when the final cut came, I was released, but they reassigned me to the practice squad. With three games left, I was activated, and I got one credited season. I played behind Pierce Holt, Mike Gann, Ricky Bryan, Jumpy Gathers, and Tim Green. I played behind a lot of guys throughout my career.

The fact that I was on the team with Bill Fralic meant that I kind of made it. When I was in college he was a legend, first at the University of Pittsburgh and then with the Falcons. And now we were playing together on the same team. I met him in a bar once in Atlanta, when I was still playing for the University of Georgia. We started talking, and he mentioned that he thought I knew his girl-friend, Mona, and much to my surprise, it was the same Mona that I thought was my girlfriend. At least he had good taste in women (I think).

Even though I was on the developmental squad, I didn't take shit from anybody. I was playing against a rookie named Robbie Tobeck (who currently plays for the Falcons), and he and I kind of clashed because we had to go against each other all the time. I remember one time we were doing a nine-on-seven drill, and he was holding me. I grabbed him by the face mask, and one thing led to another, and he ended up kicking me in the balls. I took a deep breath and just smiled at him. He looked like he saw a ghost, and just said, "Oh, shit!" and after that I think his attitude toward me changed.

Tim Green:

What the offensive linemen on our team dreaded more than anything else was to have Bill get into their pads, because if he got into their pads, he would basically just lift them off the ground and just "jackhammer" them back to the quarterback. He had incredible power, and if he got into you, pretty much IT WAS OVER! You might as well forget it, because he had great leverage and he had incredible strength. He'd just take these 300-plus, 320-pound guys, and he'd just lift them off their feet and just drive 'em straight back. It was an embarrassing thing for guys to have that happen to them. They were very attentive to trying to keep Bill away from their bodies.

Working for Jerry Glanville was great. People love him or people hate him, but I loved him. He was a defensive-minded coach, and he didn't give a shit what people thought. He spoke his mind and he was very intense and he loved loyalty. He was one cool cat. When two-a-days ended, he loaded the entire team in a bus, and we went to a bar and celebrated. He wore all black . . . what was not to like about him? Plus, he's a car buff and he races trucks. We developed a very casual rapport when I played for him, but now we've grown to be friends. His racing shop is thirty minutes from my house outside of Atlanta.

We had a lot of colorful characters on the Falcons, and Deion

That's me, Atlanta Falcon #71.

Sanders probably topped the list. It was known that Deion had forty or fifty different suits, and fifty different pairs of shoes, and fifty shirts to match. His closet looked like the rotisserie at your local professional cleaners. He was Prime Time, and he brought a lot of high-profile characters around with him. I was like one of his bodyguards, keeping people away from him when we traveled from game to game.

Chuck Smith:

We would set up some couches as the ring, and Deion Sanders was Don King. Guys would wrestle, and Goldie was always the ace in the hole. He would walk in the ring and Deion would ask, "Anybody want to mess with Goldberg?" Everybody goes, "Nah, the mother's crazy."

One time, we were on a long flight to Vegas and a few guys started up their regular poker game. M. C. Hammer was there with Deion. Hammer's a great guy, but this wasn't his lucky day. When we landed in Vegas, M.C.'s wallet was about twenty grand lighter. Go figure why he's had his share of financial problems.

There were some of the best guys I've ever met, playing for the Falcons, and I'll always be friends with a number of them.

Mike Gann Mike helped me out more than anybody else on the Falcons and for that I'll always be grateful. He gave me pointers that helped me get as far as I did with the team. That I didn't make it is no fault of his. We played a lot of golf together and we're still good friends. Mike owns a few GNCs (General Nutrition Centers) and I've been a very good customer of his for years. Mike Gann was a very solid defensive lineman even though he played college ball at Notre Dame. We all make mistakes, Mike.

Pierce Holt What a terrific guy. He had a guaranteed contract with the Falcons and he didn't miss a day of practice. There aren't many people in the world of sports, let alone the NFL, who have guaranteed contracts and still don't miss a day of practice. You won't find anybody, guaranteed contract or not, rookie or All-Pro, who works harder than Pierce Holt.

I remember one training camp where during practice, if you did something that we thought was stupid, people would label you Forrest, after the movie *Forrest Gump*. Whoever screwed up would be designated Forrest for the day, and we put it on the back of their jersey, usually without their knowing it. Pierce was a frequent recipient. On picture day, it came to our attention that his son's name was Forrest. We never knew, and of course, he never offered the information. He must have liked having his son's name on the back of his jersey, even though it was a slam.

Ricky Bryan When I was growing up playing high school football in Tulsa, I used to watch Ricky play for the University of Oklahoma. He was a defensive lineman, and he was always someone I looked up to and respected. Here I was, ten or fifteen years later, and we were playing on the same team. He was a country boy, and he reminded me of being back home in Oklahoma. In fact, when I was a bouncer at the Caravan in Tulsa, I helped throw out Ricky's brother seemingly week after week.

Jamal Anderson The memory that always sticks out in my mind is playing against Jamal Anderson when we were both on the developmental squad when he was a rookie. I used to pound him time after time, and every time he'd get right back up and run back to the huddle. I always respected him for that. He's a hell of a running back—he went from the development squad to the All-Pro team. He and I are still friends today. He comes to a lot of the matches.

Chuck Smith A passionate player. He loves what he does and he's a perfectionist. He's a good guy, although he's got a lot of nerve saying that I'm the crazy one. One practice, he got into a fight with Roman Fortin, and as Roman was walking off the field, Chuck took off his helmet and went to hit Roman in the head with it. That's kind of bogus, but that's an example of the passion that Chuck has for what he does. Though he goes about things in a different way than the norm, he loves what he does, and I love him for that.

Jessie Tuggle I will always admire Jessie because he was a hard worker and he was there year after year after year. He's still going strong. He was a little short and he didn't get the recognition he deserved, but he kept plugging and plugging and he finally made All-Pro. Man, he was stronger than hell, and he pushed me in the weight room more than anybody. He's a great guy, and to this day he brings his kids to see my matches.

Terance Mathis Also one of the great guys that I've met. He's a real quiet family guy who does more than his share for kids.

The weight coach and staff, especially the equipment manager, Whitey, were great guys, as was new head coach June Jones . . . for an offensive guy. He was mild-mannered and straight as an arrow, and he seemed to respect me for who I was and my talents and what I did for the team. In the end, he may have helped me more than I deserved.

Bill Kollar The defensive-line coach was the only person I ever met that would scream at the top of his lungs every time he opened his mouth. I'm surprised that he didn't explode. He was a good guy who was a very passionate coach and a good teacher and motivator. He was also a great player with the Cleveland Browns. I guess he made me a better player by screaming at me so damn much.

Tim Green:

We had a defensive-line coach who was really one of the best in the business, Bill Kollar. Kollar would really ride you hard. He would ride everybody. I know Kollar had a lot of respect for Bill, because as hard as he would ride him, Bill would always respond. Kollar was maniacal in his yelling and his demanding style of coaching. Whatever he demanded, Bill gave him. I think

Kollar really had a love for the guy. I can hear Kollar in my mind right now, saying, "GOOOOOLDBEEEEEEERG!" (LAUGH) He was always yelling Bill's name. He loved when Bill was successful or did something well. He would celebrate it, but he would ride him when things went wrong. He'd ride him hard. GOOOOOLDBEEEERG!! (LAUGH) He was always yelling, "GOOOOOLDBEEEERG," whether it was in praise or in castigation!

Chuck Smith (On Bill):

I think he's great. He liked to knock guys out, kick people. Now he can do it every day.

My First Heel-turn

During my first season with the Falcons, a group of us, including Harper LaBelle and Pierce Holt, went to an Atlanta Knights hockey game together. For the intermission, they asked for two volunteers to don those big, plastic, overstuffed sumo wrestling suits and go out on the rink for a mock wrestling match. Harper agreed to participate, and somehow they talked me, of all people, into it. The only problem was I had temporarily forgotten that I'm claustrophobic. As I was donning my sumo suit, a feeling of panic went through my body. By the time I got out there, man, I was dying.

Harper and I had everything planned out. We were going to make it out like a Three Stooges routine. As we were exiting the ice to a standing ovation, I made my move. The crowd loved it. Harper was in front of me and we were slipping and sliding, trying to get our footing. I was shaking my hands up in the air as if directing the crowd through a chorus of "For He's a Jolly Good Fellow," and I was getting cheers. Out of nowhere, I gave Harper a cheap shot from behind, which knocked him on his can, and I took off. The crowd went crazy. That was my first wrestling match in front of a live audience, and it was definitely the first time I ever turned on somebody.

The first two years with the Falcons were kind of a blur. The second year I was brought in again, and with the rule change, you could activate and deactivate players. I was deactivated week after week, but I played enough to qualify for another credited season. I came back for a third year and went through preseason, and I got hurt, and there you go. I was luckier than shit to get a pension.

I do have a lot of bad feelings toward the Falcons because of my injury, no question about it. I had to go through the threat of a lawsuit to resolve the matter. The basis for the lawsuit was that I felt I was misdiagnosed, and I was. They sure as hell didn't help me in my preparation for the next season, and they put me on the supplemental draft list in lieu of keeping me or getting rid of me. They knew they couldn't release me without compensation, because I was injured.

So it put a bad taste in my mouth. I guess my lack of ability overshadowed how much I sacrificed for the team. Essentially, I was being thrown away. It was all about business, and that's when I really learned what professional football was all about. They didn't think they owed me anything, and I thought they did. I sued for future medical bills, for everything I had been through, and a year's worth of care and everything associated with it. We settled the case. I got a lot less than I deserved, but it was better than nothing.

Harper LaBelle
and I go sumo.

Overall, my feelings toward the Falcons are less than rosy. But I do value the good friends I made and the good times I had there. Basically, the Falcons sucked and so did I, but it was a pretty good life.

One of the many.

NFL

NATIONAL FOOTBALL LEAGUE

NOTICE OF TERMINATION

SEPT. 5 , 1993

TO: BILL GOLDBERG

You are hereby notified that effective immediately your NFL Player Contract(s) with the Club covering the 1993 football season(s) has (have) been terminated for the reason(s) checked below:

( ) You have failed to establish or maintain your excellent physical condition to the satisfaction of the Club physician.

( ) You have failed to make full and complete disclosure of your physical or mental condition during a physical examination.

(x) In the judgment of the Club, your skill or performance has been unsatisfactory as compared with that of other players competing for positions on the Club's roster.

( ) You have engaged in personal conduct which, in the reasonable judgment of the Club, adversely affects or reflects on the Club.

ATLANTA FALCONS
Club

By: _____

PLAYER COPY

chapter fourteen

ONE BAD TURN DESERVES ANOTHER

Fast Forward

As you've already read, after the Falcons let me go to the expansion draft, I got picked up and released by the Panthers. I then told my family that I was going to become a professional wrestler and I decided to sign with the WCW. I won the U.S. Title, then the World Title, and became somewhat of a celebrity. I then lost to Nash, put my arm through the limo window, and the next thing I knew, I awoke from surgery with an arm full of torn muscles and tendons and a sliced artery. I was told before I went under that if the surgery took about an hour and a half then things would be O.K. It ended up taking three hours, so basically, I was screwed.

Before I got hurt, Lisa and I were planning to go to California anyway to spend time at my new house, and earlier in the evening we were trying to figure out the logistics. After spending the night in the hospital, the next morning I decided to charter a jet and get there as soon and as painlessly as possible. Rick Steiner came along for the ride and we stopped in Tulsa to drop him off, refuel the plane, and refuel ourselves with some burgers from one of my favorite restaurants, Goldie's (no relation). Rick's family met us at the plane and we exchanged him for the burgers.

Before we left, I told the attending physicians that I was headed to San Diego, and they did some research and gave me the name of one of the top hand surgeons in the area. They suggested that he examine me when I got there. His name was Dr. David Kupfer and, coincidentally, he and my brother Steve are surfing buddies. He conveniently arranged to check me out and change my bandages at another of my favorite restaurants, the Pacific Coast Grill in Solana Beach. After my checkup, we ordered some food to go and headed north to my new home.

DISCUSSION

I have counseled Mr. Goldberg on the need to refrain from striking objects that may result in serious injury. The injury sustained resulted in exposure of the ulnar nerve and artery. Had the penetration gone a few millimeters deeper, threatening bleeding could have ensued. In addition, had the ulnar nerve been transected, this would have resulted in paralysis of the majority of the muscles in the hand, for which function would have never been normal. This would have resulted in clawing of the fingers and an inability to fully grip using the right hand. I have discussed these candid reflections with Mr. Goldberg at length.

Here we were, Lisa and I, staying in my new house for the first time, a nice romantic vacation for a couple of days right around Christmastime, and I had just torn my arm half to shreds. I had no furniture in the house, no TV, and few utensils. Lisa had to drag the mattresses in, and fortunately, my buddy Brad Stagg came over to help us out. He helped me out a lot during my invalid stage. It sucked; I was totally dependent on Lisa and everybody else. I couldn't drive, I couldn't do shit. Fortunately, I became ambidextrous after I broke my arm playing baseball in the sixth or seventh grade.

The months preceding my injury were not the best of times for WCW. But no matter what, when you're away you want to be there, and every day I wanted to be there more and more. Though the time off was good for me in a lot of ways, it really sucked knowing I couldn't do anything about my injury. Especially since there was the possibility that I wouldn't be one hundred percent when I came back. So with each day that passed, I went deeper into depression. I couldn't work out, and working out is very important to me. I had lost the positive stimuli from wrestling. And even the most menial tasks necessary for survival required help from others. That was the hardest part, since I'm such an independent person. Not to mention that none of my cars were automatics and I couldn't drive them.

On the plus side, I didn't have the rigors and the pressure of the road, and it was great to have a break from the strain on my body and my mind. Any time you get off for a week—let alone a month, or six months—your body is going to benefit from the rest. Obviously, there are a lot of bumps you're not taking. Sometimes, though, with my personality, I fail to see the good that can surface in difficult situations. I tend to focus on the negative and don't truly take advantage of the positive side of things. Fortunately, some things occur whether you want to take advantage of them or not— like my body healing over a six-month period of time.

I didn't watch the show for a while, but once I started healing I became interested again. I started watching both WCW and World Wrestling Federation, and I tried to be impartial and see what, if anything, our shows were lacking. I looked for things that we could do to be a better show.

It was a bummer being in California but not being able to take advantage of being off of work and being outside. They had to get me off the couch with a forklift. I hadn't taken that much time off from working out since the seventh or eighth grade. It was terrific for my body, and it probably will add another year to my career, but, realistically, the injury might have taken off five. At least I got a year back.

After three months, they took my brace off and I was finally able to bend my wrist. Thanks to my buddy Matt Folts from Health South pushing my ass through a long and tedious rehab, I was able to make it back to the gym.

Although this was a low point in a lot of ways, during the time off I was able to take a really cool trip to Hawaii, thanks to my association with WCW. Lisa and I hadn't had a vacation in who knows how long. It was particularly good for us to go there, because we always try to go to a beach somewhere that we haven't been before. The last time I'd been to Hawaii was in eighth grade . . . and the girl I was with was my mom.

This time around, I was there for a Coors convention at the Orchid at Mauna Lani Hotel on the big island of Hawaii. After we checked in, the bellman directed us to our room and informed us that we were in for a special treat. We arrived at what was once Jerry Garcia's favorite suite, which was funny, because not long before, we had requested the Jerry Garcia suite in the Hotel Triton in San Francisco, per Steve's recommendation. It was an honor to be part of the Coors promotion. There were a number of people there that were legitimate superstars: Bill Russell, Willie Mays, John Elway, Ahmad Rashad (Steve's buddy from his Minnesota days), and Bobby Hull among them. Joe Montana was also a part of this promotion, and I noticed that when he walked into the room conversation ceased. He had an aura about him, and it was pretty strange. What a down-to-earth guy. I also got to hang out with Jamie Foxx, who was one funny dude and a huge wrestling fan. We also ran into Steve Young down there, and this was the first time we'd met. It turned out that he was at the resort for his wedding.

It was soothing being on the island. It was the antithesis of what

I do for work. I feel like if I don't do something that extreme, I don't get the complete relaxation I need to keep going. If we don't get to a beach every six or eight months, then I'm not recharging myself enough. I need to slow my heart rate down to almost a stop, because most of the time it's going a hundred miles an hour. That's my medicine. When we returned home after about a week, to our surprise the first pictures we saw of the trip were published in the *Examiner* tabloid.

During my time off, I was also able to take my old friends on a trip with me. I took my buddy Larry Brown to the Monster Truck championships in Vegas, where we saw the Goldberg truck conquer once again. We went on to California for his first trip to the West Coast. There we met up with Scott Adams in San Diego for a mini Bulldog reunion. So again, I was reaping some of the benefits of my job. I'm very fortunate to provide moments like these for my friends. They are the things that you dream about when you're a kid.

When I just started back working out, I received a call informing me that I was going to be on the cover of *Sports Illustrated For Kids*. Who did they line up with to appear alongside me? Well, none other than Scott Steiner, the most physically imposing guy in wrestling. I had to do that like eight days after I started training. I hadn't been to the gym for four months! Needless to say, I wasn't exactly in the best shape of my life. Boy, was that shoot a confidence builder.

Then, before I returned to the ring, I had to do another photo shoot, for *Muscular Development* magazine. Thank god I get these opportunities, but these couldn't have come at a worse time. Maybe they wanted me to pose in the *before* stage of my development. Fortunately, when the first article came out they used a cartoon drawing of me. Goldberg's Monster Workout, *yeah right.*

Coming Back

By this point, the WCW was in complete disarray. A lot had happened: Eric Bischoff had left before I was injured, and Bill Busch became the head of the company. Russo was brought in and then was gone too. There were a lot of ups and downs. I was pretty much accustomed to the ups from before, but I was always aware that there were downs in the wrestling business, as well. But I never really realized how many downs the business could have. The company went through major changes, and is still going through some bad times as I write this. Lots of back stabbing and undermining went on during these times and I don't mean just by the wrestlers.

As I said before, I was miserable while I was out, but it would have been a very stressful time to be back at work every day at that company. And staying out of that fray was one advantage of my being hurt. But in no way, shape, or form did that have any bearing on how long I was out. No matter what, I wanted to be back there from the day I got hurt. There wasn't a day that went by that I didn't feel that I could contribute in some way. The longer I was out, the more I wanted to return. I was hoping that my comeback would be a shot in the arm for the company. It was a big story to be capitalized on, and I figured that maybe it could possibly boost our ratings. So I wanted to make sure that my comeback was done right, and I wanted input, and I was constantly inquiring about their plans for me.

Then, both Vince Russo and Eric Bischoff were brought back and Bill Busch chose not to work with Bischoff. Eric and Bill couldn't coexist, so Bill went his separate way. Bischoff was going to be in charge of the creative side of WCW, along with Russo. And Brad Siegel took over the business side. I scheduled a meeting with Brad to discuss my concerns. Making money to do something that you don't feel right about doesn't make you feel good. If you don't have a smile on your face when you look in the mirror before or after work, you aren't doing the right thing. You have to change something, in spite of how much money you're being paid. It's very difficult faking happiness in real life. I'm just not that kind of guy. Even though they don't pay me for my input, I feel they should respect my opinion enough to hear me out when it concerns our future. And I appreciate the fact that they did. Maybe it went in one ear and out the other, but at least they gave me the opportunity to express my opinion.

Eric had heard what many people knew at the time, that I wasn't exactly thrilled with him both personally or professionally. I made my feelings known not for personal reasons per se, although they did have something to do with it. I wasn't sure that Eric was the solution that would propel us back to being the number one wrestling show again.

A couple of days after my meeting with Brad Siegel, Eric called me on my bat line. (Steiner, I know it was you that gave him the number, you son of a bitch.) He wanted to meet for lunch and talk about the situation. I thought that was a good idea, since I was one of the guys that could be instrumental in helping lead the company back to prosperity. Of course, my having a positive relationship with the boss would be conducive to good business, and hopefully would result in a better show. I put everything out on the table, and we came to an understanding. The past is the past and that's the way it is, and since they chose to bring Bischoff back, it was my duty to the company to try my best to go along with the decisions they made. At that time, I was committed to doing whatever they wanted, to make things work. I owed them at least that. That doesn't mean I should have to go through hell for them, though.

They said they had a plan for my comeback, but whatever plan they had was reminiscent of their plans in the past, which pretty much meant that there was no plan. Comebacks don't happen every day, and this was such a huge opportunity that it was criminal not to exploit it.

When Russo came back to WCW, he once again tried to change the direction of the program. I feel that our show made a turn for the worse. And I'm not talking about ratings, I'm talking about the content. There was more T and A, and it was more of a theatrical production instead of a theatrical/wrestling production. You can give the fans a little "ha ha," but you have to give them wrestling at the same time. I had preached to many a parent, saying, "Don't worry about watching our show, because we're a family network, and we're not going to have that kind of smut on TNT and TBS." Then, lo and behold, we were doing the kinds of things that I had preached against. That made me a hypocrite. I can deal with that, but what sickens me is that our wrestlers' children can't even watch their fathers on the show. Plus, that kind of programming gets monotonous after a while. Why try to beat someone at their own game, especially when you have to go backward morality-wise? It's not my bag of tea, by any stretch of the imagination.

I tried to let the fans know that everyone wasn't condoning that kind of behavior on the show. And I also let them know that I was going to try to change it. First and foremost, I just don't think it's good business. Our demographics may be eighteen- to thirty-five-year-old males, but some of those guys want to watch wrestling after a while. If they wanted to just watch T and A, they could watch *Baywatch.* We have a long way to go to make our show what it can and should be. It's not rocket science. You don't have to be able to solve quadratic equations to put together a wrestling show. I don't know a hell of a lot about production, and I don't know a hell of a lot about the wrestling business, but I do know a bit about entertainment. I've been around here for a little longer than a couple of months, and I think I've been fairly successful at giving people something that they want to see. It's not like we don't have the resources to put together the best combination of people to get the job done; we just don't seem able to do so. There is a time and a place for everything in wrestling today. I know the business has evolved but one thing's for sure, you must take care of the true wrestling fans—ones who want more than two girls pulling each other's hair out. And you also must respect the people who have made the business what it is today—the guys who pounded the bricks, who can be proclaimed the pioneers of wrestling's yesteryear.

My first match back was against Tank Abbott. In the month or so before my return, every week Tank would beat up an innocent bystander, until I came back and put a stop to it. I did a promo for the match the week before in Salt Lake City, and I told Tank that if he showed up in Atlanta the following week, he wasn't going to be in any shape to leave. I wrestled Tank, and during the match Rick Steiner came out and hit me in the head with a chair. Thanks, Robbie. Waiter, I'll take six stitches and a concussion with that chair shot, please. I learned some new dance steps coming out of the ring with that concussion. I could only stay out so long and I eventually came back and saved Nash later in the show.

Then they dropped the bomb on me. I received a phone call from the creative staff, and a meeting was set up to discuss the future of my character. And being the businessperson that I am, I made a decision that by no means was forced on me. I made my own decision, even though I had my doubts that this move would be a cure for the show. I played follow the leader and agreed to make the switcheroo. I was going to become a bad guy in a few weeks. Things started going downhill from there. Week after week I went out and saved Kevin, joining the two of us together.

One Bad Turn

I was excited in one respect about turning heel, but in another way I felt terrible, because I've always told people that I'd never turn. I knew in the back of my mind, though, that it was inevitable. But I didn't realize that it could come so soon. I felt as though I turned my back on the kids. If I could get the best of both worlds, though, the possibilities would be endless. Unfortunately, to be a good bad guy, you have to get everybody, including kids, to hate you. And I didn't know to what extreme I'd have to go to be an effective heel. I never envisioned that I'd be doing the things that I'm doing, but the fact is that it's a business, and I'm an actor. I have to be able to play the role, and I have to be able to give it one hundred percent. I'll go whichever way they want me to go for the betterment of the company. But I still can't compromise certain things. It doesn't matter whether or not it's a show, there are certain things that I feel very uncomfortable doing. There are boundaries that shouldn't be crossed.

I spend a lot of my time with charities and kids who have cancer. On one of our shows, I had a brutal mission to go out and destroy Hacksaw Jim Duggan, a cancer survivor. To say that they emphasized his overcoming his illness would be an understatement. That's something that I have a very big problem with. That's an extreme that we went to that I don't think was necessary. *That* was a line that I didn't think we needed to cross. And if that is the line that I need to cross to get the people to react the way we want them to react, then I have to reevaluate things. It's gotten to the point where I'm not sure I can look at myself in the mirror. As great as this life is, it's not worth resorting to that.

These guys should be creative enough to not have to resort to that stuff. They should figure out a way for people to hate me for just being a dick, not for being cruel. A lot of kids may know it's an act, but that one kid that I may have touched that has seven months to live, is it worth messing up that kid's impression of me? Maybe that's an extreme example, and maybe I take the job too seriously, and maybe that makes me unprofessional. But hey, then that's one of my flaws as a businessman. And it's not a flaw that I'm going to be ashamed of. And if that's the way it's always been in wrestling, then, hey, I'm sorry, man, I haven't always been in wrestling.

I've broken the mold in a couple of respects. I once went out there in front of a house-show audience of five thousand people to wrestle the Giant. He flicked his cigarette at my chest. Then I speared him and jackhammered him and that was it. The whole thing lasted forty-five seconds, and when I left, people stood on their feet and cheered. They didn't feel cheated at all. Hey, if that's breaking the mold, then I think that that's something to be proud of. Not to mention the fact that I didn't even have to shower afterward.

Drinking From Lord Stanley's Cup

Driving my cars, fishing in Montana the morning of a house show because I had eight hours off, and going to Hawaii with my girlfriend for a Coors promotion, those are the things that even me out. That's what Bill Goldberg does for fun. I go to the extreme to relax, and I can't find that in my local bar. These are dreams of mine that are being fulfilled from this strange job, which at times is not so bad after all.

I had followed the NHL playoffs and when Dallas made it to the Stanley Cup Finals, I plotted out all of the games on my schedule. It wasn't feasible for me to go to any of the games before game six and, since Dallas was down three games to one, there was a chance they wouldn't make it that far. Game five was on a Thursday, and I was hoping and praying that they would win. And they did win— an unbelievable game—in the third overtime. And who tipped in the winning goal? My buddy Brett Hull. I picked up the phone and called Steve (who knew it was me), and I asked if he was going to meet me in Dallas. I didn't care if I had to wash Brett's car for tickets, I was going to be there.

Brett is a good friend of mine, and I'm very appreciative of the person that he is. He's also come through for me with tickets to some very exciting games. On this occasion, he put Steve, my friend Ross Foreman, and me in seats next to his wife, Allison. We had a great view, and it was a thrill just to be there. We had an awesome time at the game, and it looked like they were going to win, but unfortunately, they lost in the second overtime. It was a great game nonetheless. We followed Allison to the Stars lounge and we sat somberly waiting for Brett. I felt bad being around and trying to make him jovial when I knew it wasn't going to happen. We drank

**Steve and me
at the Stanley Cup Finals 2000.**

a couple of beers, conversed for a while, thanked Brett, and we were on our way.

The path to our limo took us by the locker room of the Stanley Cup champions, the New Jersey Devils. As we passed the celebration, I saw a couple of the guys hanging out outside the locker room. Out of nowhere, Calder Trophy (Rookie of the Year) winner Scott Gomez yelled, "Goldberg!" I thought "Oh shit," because as much as I wanted to go in there, I felt guilty immediately. It wasn't "Oh boy, let's go in there and party," it was "Oh no, Brett's going to see me and be pissed." But in the end, I went in. It's not like Brett wouldn't go to a WWF show.

Well, the next thing I know, I'm in the locker room and Gomez takes off my Stars hat and replaces it with his own. He even went so far as to give me the shirt off his back. They were doing some seri-

Scott Stevens, making me look small.

The experience of a lifetime. Thanks, Gomez.

Is that beer?

ous celebrating, and I was right in the middle of it. It went by so fast, it was like a dream. I didn't know what hit me. It was like they were looking outside for entertainment, and what better person than a comic-book guy like me. It was a hell of an honor, and it was great, and although I felt sorry for my friends on the Stars, it was an opportunity that could never happen again. I mean, what are the chances of that happening? It's just evidence of how lucky I am. I was in the right place at the right time, and that's happened to me more than once in my life. I not only got to have my picture taken with most of the players and the coveted Stanley Cup, but I got to drink from it! God knows what was in the Cup, but it could have been piss and it still would have been good drinking from that thing. That was awesome, man, it was the Stanley Cup! I was actually hanging with the guys that won it, and on top of that, they're fans of mine. I mean, what have I done? What did I do to deserve to be in there?

Heel Me

It's just a shame that it's one extreme or the other in this business. You're either really happy to get an opportunity like drinking from the Stanley Cup or you're really bummed out, and it shouldn't be like that. But hey, it's business, and if I can control it a little, then I'm going to make the best of it.

After the Stanley Cup game we flew to Baltimore for the *Great American Bash,* and I was about to become the great American basher. The only time I had ever been booed in wrestling (from the majority of the fans) was when I was up in Canada. But the funny thing about it was that part of me loved it. It sent a charge through my body, and it was awesome. Getting booed made me feel like ripping my opponent's head right off his neck. So when I first thought about turning heel, I just focused on that feeling, that charge, and I really didn't think about how bad it was going to feel overall.

I turned on Kevin during his match with Jeff Jarrett and joined up with Bischoff and Russo and the New Blood. I stood there amidst the flying boos and beers, and it felt kind of cool, you know, having people throw things at me. But I could look out there and see kids going "Ah, man, what's going on?" The problem is that I just don't have the conviction to try and make kids hate me. And you're doing your character an injustice if you don't have conviction with your role. And if I have to have constraints on my character to curtail the kind of bad guy I am, then I don't think that I'm fulfilling my responsibilities. But I'm trying to deal with it, and I'm trying to make the best of it. Hey, it's professional wrestling, and you never know when you'll get to the next turn.

Making a Difference

I will always do my best to make a positive difference in this business. I'm not content going out and fulfilling my minimum days'

obligations and taking my check and cashing it and going home. I'm an active participant, and I want to try and make a difference in whatever I do in life. Just making it to a certain level fame-wise or monetarily is not good enough for me. So I'm always going to be opinionated and I'm not always going to be right, but I like to think that I know what I'm doing. I'm appreciative of people listening to my opinions. But I promise you that I will not go quietly.

There are a lot of situations where guys are held hostage by the business, and there are a lot of wrongs being done. There are a lot of guys out there who can't fend for themselves, and they need a higher power to look after them. And I feel that it's my duty to try and help on some level. A prime example was a young guy on *Nitro*

Joining up with Vince Russo and Eric Bischoff.
A night to remember . . . or forget.

A little heat.

the other night that recently came out of the Power Plant. He's been wrestling on TV for a couple of months. He's athletic and he has a good gimmick. He'd do anything for the company. During his match, he flew off the top rope onto the floor outside, crushing a chair and landing on his ass. Despite being injured, he got up, got back into the ring, and finished the match. He was helped to the back and a number of people helped him backstage where he was pissing blood. They took him to the hospital for a CAT scan to see if his pelvis was broken and his spleen was all right. They had to put in a catheter to drain the blood from his kidneys, and the kid looked up, very emotional, and the first damn words out of his mouth were "They're going to cut my pay, aren't they?" That was the first damn thing out of his mouth.

We've got a guy working right now with three compressed verte-brae, and he can barely turn his neck. He has a clause in his contract that states that if he's out of wrestling for thirty days, they can fire him. What kind of crap is that? That sucks, and if that's the world we live in, then something's wrong. We have no governing body to watch over us and it pisses me off. It's hard to be a part of something like that. Until people make a concerted effort to change some of these things, this business is going to continue being a circus. It's hard to be someone who's got it good and not feel a little bit guilty about the way things are for these other guys.

It's just like football was. No matter how hard you work and how much you sacrifice your body, you can get hurt and get dropped—just like that. I've been on both sides of it, and that's why I'm so appreciative for what I have. It's why I'm so concerned for these other guys. And I'll always try to fight for them.

What's Next?

Each day brings something different—and in this business, it brings something strange. So I'd like to continue wrestling, I'd like to ful-fill my obligations with WCW, I'd like to continue to prosper in this business, and I'd love to segue into movies. There's no question that it would make me a better businessman to use my mind a little bit more and my body a little bit less. This would extend my career beyond a couple more years. But I'm addicted to wrestling right now, and with the bad does come a lot of good. I'd like to think that I'm making a difference both in the wrestling world and in the world of reality, as goofy as they both are.

Disclaimer

My life is just a story that's been told, and this is but one man's rendition of his long, strange journey. As you pass through life, there are many warnings along the way, and the one best suited for this saga is, "Don't try this at home." If you do choose to follow in my footsteps, be sure to wear a D.O.T.-approved helmet. Because it's a bumpy ride.

Bill Goldberg's Philosophy

Live life to the fullest.

There's a time and a place for everything.

Never give less than your best at all times.

Respect others, treat people like you want to be treated.

Always have time for others.

Help people who are less fortunate than you.

Kill people with kindness—until they stab you in the back,

and then just kill them (not literally).

Stop and smell the roses.

The Book

A couple of years ago, we were cruising at 39,000 feet. Mike was at the controls of his Citation X, and Steve and I were in the back sipping on a couple of cold beers. "Dude," Steve said, "you're living the American dream, and someone should write a book about it. And that someone should be me." I thought about it for half a minute, and I grinned, thinking about what a wacky idea it was. "Why not?" I said. "That's a great idea. We'll go to Cabo and write it on the beach. And visit our good friend Don Julio."

Well, we've been down to Mexico, but we didn't do much writing. We have, though, consulted frequently with our good friend Don Julio.

Steve and I spent countless hours on airplanes, in automobiles, on boats, in hotel rooms on the road, at home in California, and on the phone, compiling the information for this book. Last night, we had our final conversation and it ended like this:

"Well, Billy," Steve said, "I'll be damn glad when this book project is over."

"It is," I said, "thank god."

Acknowledgments

Special Acknowledgments

Writing this book has been a family endeavor. I, of course, provided the subject matter, Mike contributed quite a few photographs, Jed wrote a chapter, and Steve put it all together on paper. And a special thanks goes to my mother, because obviously, without her, there would be no book. Our sister, Barbara, deserves a lot of credit too. In addition to her helping recall my childhood, she married a very talented guy by the name of Larry Burnett.

Larry is not only one hell of a sportscaster, but a very accomplished sports journalist as well. He provided literary input and interviewed most of the wrestlers and celebrities for the book. This in itself was a very time-consuming task, and tracking everyone down is another story altogether.

Thanks, Larry—we couldn't have done it without you.

P.S. When does the fun begin?

Bill Goldberg's Acknowledgments

I want to thank everybody who's stuck with me my entire life. I wouldn't be who I am without my two parents, who are the best parents in the world, even though they're a bit goofy at times. I want to thank my brothers and sister just for being who they are and for the things that I've learned from them.

There's no question that my friends deserve thanks for always being there for me and for just being my friends. You guys know who you are, you sons of bitches.

A special thanks goes to my girlfriend, Lisa. She was in this business before me and she prepared me for what to expect. Being Bill Goldberg's girlfriend sure as hell ain't easy. Without her I just wouldn't be the same.

Thanks to my lifelong buddy Terry, who holds down the fort in Atlanta while I'm gone. Love you, man.

Thanks to everybody who's helped me in the wrestling business and helped mold me as a wrestler and a person. I want to thank all of the refs and the crew who put the shows on night after night, across the country. Thank you, Doug Dellinger; you've always been there for me. And thanks to the rest of the security guys: Buzz Boothe, Chris Leebrick, and Chris Couch. Thanks to Zane Bresloff, for everything.

Thanks to my managers, Barry Bloom and Michael Braverman, and their loyal assistant, Jennifer Chatien, who has definitely put in a lot of overtime because of me. Thanks also to my attorneys, Henry Holmes and John Taylor, and the people at NKS management. Without all of these people, my life would be in total disarray.

This book wouldn't be possible without my agent, Matt Bialer, from William Morris in New York, and Pete Fornatale from Crown. I thank you guys for having the confidence in my story and my profession. Thanks to everyone at Crown Publishers who helped make this book happen, especially Amy Boorstein, Lauren Dong, Leta Evanthes, and Jean Lynch. And thanks to Scott Keith, Warren Meyers, Rob Neyer, and Frank Scatoni for your help. Thanks to David Arnold for the back cover idea.

I am eternally grateful for all of the doctors who have put me back together throughout my athletic career. Most recently, Dr. Robert J. Davis, who did a fine job repairing my shredded forearm.

Thank you, Barbara, for taking care of the West Coast Goldberg Fan Club, and you too, Gloria, for taking care of the East Coast.

Gloria LaFlamme helps me out in many ways and keeps me in touch with a lot of the kids I've become friends with. Her help is invaluable and very much appreciated.

I especially want to thank all of the fans for sticking with me. I applaud and very much appreciate the passion of wrestling fans today. I'm trying to carry on the wrestling tradition, I'm not trying to change it. And a thanks to all of the cyber-fans that care enough to have created their own Goldberg Web sites.

Oh, and screw all you people who didn't have the confidence in me in the past. You know who you are as well.

And by the way, if there are any people out there who I've left out, I am forever sorry. Throughout this process, it has been very difficult trying to include everyone, so please understand. If I've misrepresented anyone because of factual inaccuracies, I'm sorry. I've been hit in the head way too many times and I've head-butted way too many lockers to remember everything exactly as it took place.

Steve Goldberg's Acknowledgments

I want to thank my wife for putting up with me and my all-night and weekend writing sessions. And for not divorcing me. I want to thank my dogs for adjusting to an ever-changing walk routine and my cat for keeping me company.

I also want to thank my partners, Mikey and Phil, and the top guys, Wolfie, Billy, John, and the rest of the managers, for picking up the slack during my short and intense literary career.

And thank you, Matt and Pete, for believing that I could actually pull this off. You're the best agent and editor dudes in the galaxy and I really, really appreciate your help. And I can't forget to thank Mr. Special Stipulation himself, Alan Wilensky.

Photo Credits

Photo Insert